Glenda W9-DFG-376

Horizons Literature

Stella Sands

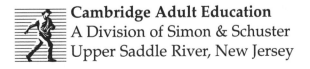
Cambridge Adult Education
A Division of Simon & Schuster
Upper Saddle River, New Jersey

Executive Director: Mark Moscowitz
Project Editors: Robert McIlwaine, Bernice Golden, Keisha Carter, Laura Baselice, Lynn Kloss
Writer: Stella Sands
Series Editor: Roberta Mantus
Consultants/Reviewers: Marjorie Jacobs, Cecily Kramer Bodnar
Production Manager: Penny Gibson
Production Editor: Nicole Cypher
Marketing Manager: Will Jarred
Interior Electronic Design: Flanagan's Publishing Services, Inc.
Illustrator: Andre V. Malok
Photo Research: Jenifer Hixson
Electronic Page Production: Flanagan's Publishing Services, Inc.
Cover Design: Armando Baez

Copyright ©1996 by Cambridge Adult Education, a division of Simon & Schuster, 1 Lake Street, Upper Saddle River, New Jersey 07458. All rights reserved. No part of this book may be reproduced or transmitted in any form or by any means, electrical or mechanical, including photocopying, recording, or by any information storage and retrieval system without permission in writing from the publisher.

Printed in the United States of America.
1 2 3 4 5 6 7 8 9 10 99 98 97 96 95
ISBN: 0-8359-4632-0

 Cambridge Adult Education
A Division of Simon & Schuster
Upper Saddle River, New Jersey

Acknowledgments

Photo Credits: p.4: The Bettmann Archive; p.7: Lawrence Migdale; p.8: Ruben Guzman; p.9: Scott J. Witte, The Picture Cube; p.10: Rick Friedman, Picture Cube; p.13: Springer/Bettmann Film Archive; p.16: Spencer Grant, The Picture Cube; p.18: Gloria Karlson, Picture Cube; p.22: Photofest; p.24: Photofest; p.25: Jack Vartoogian; p.27: Jack Vartoogian; p.30: Photofest; p.31: Photofest; p.34: Library of Congress; p.38: The Granger Collection; p.39: The Bettmann Archive; p.47: AP/Wide World Photos; p.51: AP/World Wide Photos; p.52: Steve Takatsuno, The Picture Cube; p.59: Jenifer Hixson; p.62: Spencer Grant, The Picture Cube; p.64: Photofest; p.67: Photofest; p.68: Photofest; p.70: WideWorld Photos; p.72: Courtesy of Wilma B. Carter, The Yale Repertory Theater; p.74: Scott and Gillian Aldrich; p.74: Courtesy of The Nassau Department of General Services; p.76: The Bettmann Archive; p.84: The Bettmann Archive; p.92: The Bettmann Archive; p.92: The Granger Collection; p.96: Scott and Gillian Aldrich; p.97: The Bettmann Archive; p.101: Michael Newman, Photo Edit

Literature Acknowledgments: "Fame is Bee" by Emily Dickinson. Reprinted by permission of the publishers and the Trustees of Amherst College from THE POEMS OF EMILY DICKINSON, Thomas H. Johnson, ed., Cambridge, Mass.: The Belknap Press of Harvard University Press, Copyright © 1951, 1955, 1979, 1983 by the President and Fellows of Harvard College. "Arithmetic" from THE COMPLETE POEMS OF CARL SANDBURG, copyright 1950 by Carl Sandburg and renewed 1978 by Margaret, Helga Sandburg Crile, and Janet Sandburg, reprinted by permission of Harcourt Brace & Company. "Hope" is the Thing With Feathers" by Emily Dickinson, Public Domain. "Hope" from THE POEMS OF EMILY DICKINSON, The Belknap Press of Harvard University Press. "Harriet Tubman" by Eloise Greenfield from HONEY, I LOVE by Eloise

(continued on page 124)

Contents

Unit
1

Nonfiction

Speech

What You Know   Have you ever listened to a speech? Perhaps you heard the President speak on TV. Maybe a well-known person from your community spoke at a meeting. A speech expresses the ideas and feelings of the speaker. It can show the ability of the speaker to use the spoken word.

Below is part of a speech given by a Native American, Chief Joseph of the Nez Percé (nehz-PUHRS) tribe, in 1877. It is a speech in which Chief Joseph says that he and his tribe give up and will no longer fight the U.S. Army. The army was taking away tribal lands in Oregon.

As you read the speech, say each word carefully, as if you were giving this speech in front of several hundred people.

> I am tired of fighting. Our chiefs are killed. Looking Glass is dead. . . . The old men are all dead. . . . It is cold and we have no blankets. The little children are freezing to death. My people, some of them, have run away to the hills and have no blankets, no food; no one knows where they are—perhaps freezing to death.

Sometimes when you listen to a speech, you hear words you have never heard before. The same is true when you are reading and see a word you have never seen before. When this happens, see whether it is like other words you already know. Then say the new word the way you say the other words.

How It Works

Almost every word in the English language has at least one **vowel** (VOW-uhl) in it. The vowels are a, e, i, o, and u. Each vowel can be said in two different ways.

Say the words *we* and *children*. The *e* in *we* sounds just like the letter *e* in the alphabet. Vowels that are said the way they sound in the alphabet have **long vowel sounds**. Here are more examples of words with long vowel sounds:

a as in *save*	*e* as in *freezing*	*i* as in *tired*
o as in *old*	*u* as in *useless*	

Try It

Here are more sentences from Chief Joseph's speech. Some of the underlined words have long vowel sounds. Write only these words in the answer blanks.

I am tired; my heart <u>is</u> <u>sick</u> and <u>sad</u>.

From where the <u>sun</u> now stands I will <u>fight</u> <u>no</u> more forever.

_____ _____

The *i* in *fight* is a long *i*. The *o* in *no* is a long *o*. The *i* in *is* and *sick* does not sound like the letter *i* in the alphabet. The *a* in *sad* is also not said the way an *a* is said in the alphabet. The *u* in *sun* is not said the way it is in the alphabet.

How It Works

Some vowels are not said the way they sound when you say the alphabet aloud. In the word *is*, the letter *i* does not sound like the letter *i* in the alphabet. Words that have these kinds of sounds have **short vowel sounds**.

Here are some examples of words that have short vowel sounds:

a as in *sad*   *e* as in *them*   *i* as in *will*

o as in *from*   *u* as in *sun*

Try It

Here is another sentence from Chief Joseph's speech. Some of the underlined words have short vowel sounds. Write only these words in the blanks.

<u>Tell</u> General Howard I <u>know</u> <u>his</u> heart.

_____ _____

The *e* in *tell* has a short *e* sound. The *i* in *his* is a short *i*. The *o* in *know* is a long *o*.

Chief Joseph gave a powerful speech about how awful war is.

Practice

Below are two more sentences from Chief Joseph's speech:

It is the young men who say yes and no. He who led on the young men is dead.

I want to have time to look for my children and see how many I can find.

Look at the *first vowel* in each underlined word above. Write *long* on the answer blank if the vowel is long. Write *short* if the vowel is short.

1. is _____

5. children _____

2. no _____

6. see _____

3. led _____

7. find _____

4. time _____

Check your answers on page 117.

Follow-Up

Imagine that you are giving a speech about war. What might your first sentence be? Write this sentence. Then count how many long vowel sounds and how many short vowel sounds there are in your sentence.

Biography

What You Know Is there someone famous whose life you would like to know more about? Some people are interested in the lives of political leaders. They might read a book about the life of Malcolm X, Abraham Lincoln, or Bill Clinton. Others like to find out about what happened in the lives of sports stars. These people might choose a book about Michael Jordan, Mickey Mantle, or Joe Louis.

A book that is written about the life of someone is called a **biography** (beye-AHG-ruh-fee). Biographies are written not only about famous people. They can be written about people whose lives are especially interesting even though they are not famous.

For example, a biography could be written about someone who made an exciting escape from a prisoner-of-war camp. A biography also could be written about a person who left his or her home to escape to freedom in another country. Biographies are written about all kinds of people from all over the world. They tell about interesting or unusual lives.

Here is part of a biography written about Sandra Cisneros. Have you ever heard of her? She is a Mexican-American writer who grew up poor in Chicago. She writes about her experiences growing up as a Mexican American.

In the following paragraph, you will see two words followed by stars (*). You will see other words followed by stars throughout this book. Words followed by stars are defined at the end of this book, starting on page 113.

Sometimes you will see names that you have never seen before. When this happens, you can sound out the letters to figure out how to say the new name.

As you read the paragraph below, say each word out loud. Pronounce the underlined words especially carefully.

> One day her <u>classmates</u> were discussing their childhood homes. Cisneros had always been embarrassed by the shabby,* cramped* houses and apartments her family had lived in. At first, <u>Cisneros</u> thought that this discussion only <u>proved</u> that she didn't belong.

Words with astericks (*) are defined in the Word List on pages 113-116.

How It Works

In Lesson 1 you learned about the sounds of vowels: a, e, i, o, u. In this lesson, you will learn about the sounds of the other letters of the alphabet. These letters are called **consonants** (KAHN-suh-nuhnts). The consonants are:

b, c, d, f, g, h, j, k, l, m, n, p, q, r, s, t, v, w, x, y, and z

Look at the first two letters at the beginning of each word below:

day   **di**scussing   **fa**mily   **be**long

Each word starts with a single consonant followed by a vowel. The word *day* begins with the consonant *d*. It is followed by the vowel *a*. The word *discussing* begins with the consonant *d*. It is followed by the vowel *i*. The word *family* begins with the consonant *f*. It is followed by the vowel *a*. The word *belong* begins with the consonant *b*. It is followed by the vowel *e*.

Now look at the first two letters at the beginning of each of these words:

classmates

cramped

proved

Each word starts with two consonants.

cl

cr

pr

Each consonant has its own sound, and you can hear that sound when you say the word. When the consonants are together, they are said very quickly so that they form almost one sound. Pairs of consonants like these are called **consonant blends**.

Say *classmates, cramped,* and *proved* out loud slowly. Then say them quickly. Don't the consonants at the beginning of each word make almost one sound?

Children all over the world do the same kinds of things. They love to play.

Try It

In this picture there are several children who are wearing skirts. They are playing in a yard. Circle the consonant blends at the beginning of each of these words:

skirts

playing

The consonant blends are **sk** in *skirts* and **pl** in *playing*. Each consonant has its own sound. Both consonants are said quickly so that they form almost one sound.

Read this sentence from the biography of Sandra Cisneros. Some words begin with consonant blends. Underline the consonant blends.

Born in 1954 into a family of six brothers, she was protected, sometimes too much so.

How many consonant blends are there? There are two. They begin the words **br**others and **pr**otected. The *sh* in *she* is not a consonant blend. The *s* and the *h* are not said separately at all. They go together to form a new, different sound. This is also the case for *th* and *ch*. Can you think of any others?

Now read this sentence and underline the consonant blends.

He was angry and puzzled* that his good Mexican daughter felt she had to move away from his protection.

The consonant blends begin the words **fr**om and **pr**otection.

Sandra Cisneros writes stories about the experiences of Mexican Americans.

Practice

Read these sentences. Some words *begin* with consonant blends.
Underline the consonant blends at the beginning of words.

1. Sandra Cisneros has a pretty smile on her face.

2. The Cisneros family often traveled back and forth from
Mexico to the United States.

3. One of Cisneros's books is called *The House on Mango
Street*.

4. Her stories tell of poor people who have too little space
in which to live.

5. Cisneros feels proud that her words can make people
laugh and cry.

Check your answers on page 117.

Follow-Up

How many of your friends, family members, and classmates were not born in
the United States? Make a list of them. Then count how many of their names
begin with consonant blends.

Autobiography

What You Know

Suppose you meet someone who asks you to tell her about your life. You might begin by telling her when and where you were born. Perhaps you could tell a story about your early childhood. You could describe a special success or a tragedy that took place.

If you were to write that information in a book, it would be called an **autobiography** (aw-toh-beye-AHG-ruh-fee). An autobiography is a story of a person's life written by that person.

In Jade Snow Wong's autobiography, *Fifth Chinese Daughter*, she tells her

All people have interesting stories to tell about their lives.

feelings about being born Chinese. Here are a few sentences about the Chinese New Year from her autobiography. Pay special attention to the underlined words as you read the sentences out loud.

> The Wong children, all scrubbed with their hair washed, were dressed in new clothes, for New Year's literally meant that everything should be new, renewed, or clean.
> It was also poor taste to talk about unpleasant subjects, such as death, for that would also bring bad luck . . .

You may not be aware of it, but you know word beginnings that change the meaning of words. For example, you know that the word beginning *un* changes the word *happy* to *unhappy*—a word with a whole different meaning.

How It Works

Ms. Wong writes that, during the Chinese New Year, everything should be *renewed*. No one should talk about *unpleasant* subjects. The words *renew* and *unpleasant* have **prefixes** (PREE-fiks-ihz). A prefix is one or more letters added to the beginning of a word. By adding a new word-beginning, you can change the meaning of the word.

For example, by adding the prefix *re* to the word *new*, you make another word. *Renew* means to make new again. The prefix *re* means *again* (*renew* = again + new).

The prefix *un* before a word gives that word the opposite meaning. So *unpleasant* means the opposite of *pleasant*. It means *not pleasant* (*unpleasant* = not + pleasant).

Try It

Let's look at three more prefixes: *non*, *mis*, and *pre*. *Non* means "not." A *nonsmoker* is someone who does not smoke. *Nonsense* is something that does not make sense. *Mis* means "wrong or not right." *Misbehavior* means behavior that is wrong. *Misread* means to "read something the wrong way." *Pre* means "before." *Predawn* comes before sunrise (dawn). *Preholiday* means "before a holiday."

Put a check mark next to the words that complete the following sentences correctly.

1. A costume for the New Year's celebration that can't be found is a

__ preplaced costume __ misplaced costume __ nonplaced costume

The correct answer is *misplaced costume*. The costume hasn't been placed before. The costume isn't one that has not been placed. The costume has been put in the wrong place.

Chinese New Year is celebrated with a lion dance on the street.

2. A time for guests to arrive which has been set up ahead of time is a

___ prearranged time ___ misarranged time ___ nonarranged time

The correct answer is *prearranged*. The time wasn't set up in a wrong way. The time isn't one that was not arranged. It's a time that was set up earlier, before the guests arrived.

3. Some people cook food for the Chinese New Year in a pan to which food does not stick. In that case, the food is cooked in a

___ prestick pan ___ misstick pan ___ nonstick pan

The correct answer is *nonstick pan*. The pan isn't one to which the food sticks before you cook it. It isn't one to which the food sticks incorrectly. It is a pan to which the food does not stick.

Practice

Circle the prefix in each underlined word. Then put a check mark next to the correct meaning of the prefix.

1. Some people <u>misunderstand</u> the meaning of the Chinese New Year.

_____ wrong   _____ again   _____ before

2. Chinese New Year is a seven-day celebration. It is <u>unlike</u> the New Year's celebration in the United States.

_____ before   _____ wrong   _____ not

3. Some people <u>preset</u> their tables with dishes, knives, and forks.

_____ before   _____ again   _____ not

4. For seven days, there are <u>nonstop</u> celebrations.

_____ before   _____ not   _____ again

Check your answers on page 117.

Follow-Up

Write the first paragraph of your autobiography.

Diary

What You Know Do you write your thoughts and feelings in a **diary** (DEYE-uh-ree)? If so, do you let anyone else read what you have written? Many diaries are read only by the people who write them. Some diaries, however, are read by others.

Anne Frank was a young girl who wrote in her diary while her family was in hiding during World War II. The Franks were Jewish, and the Nazis* had invaded their home in the Netherlands.* In time, most Jews, as well as many non-Jewish people, were taken away to concentration camps,* where they died.

Anne's diary was published as a book titled *The Diary of a Young Girl*. It has been read by millions of people all over the world. Anne's story is one of courage in the face of great danger.

Here is a short part of the diary, which was written during the two years she hid in a small room directly under the roof of a Dutch* family's home.

> And as for us, we are fortunate. Yes, we are luckier than millions of people. It is quiet and safe here. . . . We are even so selfish as to talk about "after the war," brighten up at the thought of having new clothes and new shoes, whereas we really ought to save every penny, to help other people, and save what is left from the wreckage* after the war.
>
> The children here run about in just a thin blouse and clogs*; no coat, no hat, no stockings, and no one helps them. Their tummies are empty, they chew an old carrot to stay the pangs,* go from their cold homes out into the cold street and, when they get to school, find themselves in an even colder classroom.

Anne Frank's writing is powerful. The words she chooses clearly express what is happening. Two words in this section mean the same thing: *fortunate* and *lucky*. Two words, *new* and *old*, are opposites.

How It Works

Two words that mean the same thing are called **synonyms** (SIHN-uh-nihmz), for example, *happy* and *glad*. Two words that have opposite meanings are **antonyms** (AN-tuh-nihmz), such as *cold* and *hot*.

Anne Frank's diary tells about her life in hiding during World War II.

Anne Frank's diary is a record of her life in Holland* between 1942 and 1944. Here are a few more sentences from the diary. Look at the underlined words. The underlined word in the first sentence—*forbidden*—means "not allowed."

1. Jews are <u>forbidden</u> to visit theaters.

2. Most sports grounds are <u>prohibited</u> to them.

3. Jews are <u>banned</u> from taking trains.

4. Jews are <u>allowed</u> to do their shopping only between 3 and 5 o'clock.

In sentence 2, the word *prohibited* is used. It means the same as *forbidden*. *Forbidden* and *prohibited* are synonyms; they both mean "not allowed." Sentence 3 uses a synonym for both *forbidden* and *prohibited*. This synonym, *banned*, also means "not allowed." Sentence 4 says that Jews are *allowed* to shop only at certain hours. *Allowed* is an antonym for *prohibited*, *forbidden*, and *banned*. It means the opposite of these words.

Try It

Here is more information about Anne Frank. Read the sentences. Look carefully at the underlined word in the first sentence.

1. On August 4, 1944, the German secret police <u>discovered</u> the hiding place of the Franks.

2. On August 4, 1944, the German secret police <u>found</u> the hiding place of the Franks.

3. On August 4, 1944, the German secret police <u>overlooked</u> the hiding place of the Franks.

Which word is a synonym for the word *discovered*?

_____

Found is a synonym for *discovered*. *Found* means the same thing as *discovered*.

Which word is an antonym for *discovered*? _____

Overlooked is an antonym for *discovered*. *Overlooked* means the opposite of *discovered*.

Now read these sentences. Look carefully at the underlined word in the first sentence.

1. Anne Frank wrote that in spite of* everything she still believed that people are really <u>good</u> at heart.

2. Anne Frank wrote that in spite of everything she still believed that people are really <u>well-meaning</u> at heart.

3. Anne Frank wrote that in spite of everything people are really not <u>bad</u> at heart.

Which word is a synonym for *good*? _____

Well-meaning is a synonym for *good*. *Well-meaning* means the same as *good*.

Which word is an antonym for the word *good*? _____

Bad is an antonym for *good*. It means the opposite of *good*.

Practice

Read the following sentences and look at the underlined words. Then answer the questions.

1. Anne Frank sometimes told <u>sad</u> stories. Very little news was cheerful. One depressing story she told was of seeing her many Jewish friends being taken away. They were loaded into cattle cars.

   a. Which word is a synonym for *sad*? _____

   b. Which word is an antonym for *sad*? _____

2. Anne and her family had to be <u>quiet</u> most of the time while they were in hiding. If they were noisy, they might be discovered. Often, they were so silent that one could hear a pin drop.

   a. Which word is a synonym for *quiet*? _____

   b. Which word is an antonym for *quiet*? _____

3. Both older and younger people had a <u>difficult</u> time living in the small hiding place. It was especially hard for the older people. Nobody found life easy during those years.

   a. Which word is a synonym for *difficult*? _____

   b. Which word is an antonym for *difficult*? _____

Check your answers on page 117.

Follow-Up

Try writing a diary for a week. You might write about things you do and events that happen. You should also write about what you think and feel.

News Story

What You Know   Do you like hot weather? How does 85 degrees sound to you? What about 90 degrees? Do you prefer cold weather? Maybe 40 degrees sounds just right.

Most people find it difficult to carry on their normal lives when temperatures get too hot or too cold. Read this news story about a heat wave. News stories give facts about events that are taking place. Have you ever experienced temperatures like those described in this news story?

Chicago Holds On

Temperatures rose to almost 100 degrees again today. A heat emergency has been declared. Rescue crews are knocking on doors to help the elderly.

This is being done to avoid what happened earlier this month. Then, temperatures reached 106 degrees. The heat was blamed for causing more than 500 deaths.

Some people can put up with very high temperatures for a day or two. However, when it stays hot for a long time, the body's defenses are worn down.

Extreme heat is causing trouble all over the country. In Arizona some workers fainted after the heat reached 110 degrees. Heat-damaged tracks caused a train accident in Indiana. Here in Chicago, people are being told to go to "cooling centers." These centers are places set up to help those without air conditioning.

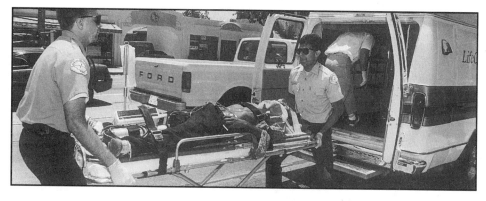

Newspapers often print information about what happens during heat waves.

When you read a news story, you may see words that you have never seen before. You can figure out how to say them by sounding out the letters in the words.

How It Works

In Lesson 1, you learned about the sounds of the vowels:

a, e, i, o, and u

In Lesson 2, you learned about the consonants:

b, c, d, f, g, h, j, k, l, m, n, p, q, r, s, t, v, w, x, y, and z

Take a moment now to look back at Lesson 2. It is about words that start with consonant blends. Consonant blends are made up of two consonants. Each consonant has its own sound. When you say the two consonants together quickly they almost form one sound. Some examples in Lesson 2 were **cl**assmates, **cr**amped, and **pr**oved. These words have consonant blends at the beginning of each word.

This lesson is about words that *end* in consonant blends. Here are some words from the news story that end in consonant blends:

almost	worn	help
down	told	

Say these words out loud. The last two letters are pronounced together. Each consonant has its own sound. However, when you say them together quickly, the two sounds form almost one sound.

Here are other examples of words that end in consonant blends:

Word	Consonant Blend
sound	nd
stamp	mp
start	rt

Try It

Circle the consonant blends at the *end* of these words:

left   front   behind   past

The consonant blends are **ft** in *left*, **nt** in *front*, **nd** in *behind*, and **st** in *past*.

News stories give information about everyday events—even record-breaking temperatures.

Read these sentences. Circle the consonant blends at the end of words.

1. Some people make the best of a hot day.

2. They swim or surf in the ocean.

How many consonant blends are there? There are two. They are at the end of the words be**st** and su**rf**. Say these words out loud.

Now read these sentences. Circle the consonant blends at the ends of words.

1. Some children get cool in the water from a fire hydrant.

2. People like to have a cold drink.

3. A fan often does not help.

4. It can blow the hot air around.

5. Extreme heat and humidity can cause death to occur.

Did you find the words that end with consonant blends? They are hydra**nt**, co**ld**, dri**nk**, he**lp**, arou**nd**, and a**nd**. You may have guessed that *death* ends in a consonant blend. However, the two consonants, *t* and *h*, do not form a consonant blend. When you say *t* and *h* together, a new sound is formed.

Practice

Read these sentences. Some words *end* in consonant blends. Write these words in the answer blanks. Then circle the consonant blends in the words you have written.

1. In a newspaper, you can read about a local event that is of special interest to you.

_____

2. Different people may have one section of the paper that they like the best.

_____   _____

3. The work of a cartoonist may be seen in many cities.

_____   _____

4. Important stories are on the front page.

_____   _____

Check your answers on page 117.

Follow-Up

Cut out a short article from your local newspaper. Circle the consonant blends at the beginnings and ends of words.

Unit
2

Commentary on the Arts

TV Shows

What You Know What kinds of TV shows do you like to watch? Do you enjoy game shows, soap operas, or news and weather reports? Some people like to watch sports on TV. Others enjoy seeing true stories about people and animals.

In many newspapers and magazines, reviewers* write about TV shows. If you read this review* of "Murder, She Wrote," do you think you would tune in to see it?

Solving Mysteries* the Nonviolent Way

"Murder, She Wrote" does not have much violence in it. There aren't any special effects. Wild car chases and shoot-outs don't happen very often. So what makes this mystery show so popular? The answer is two words: Jessica Fletcher.

Jessica is the charming* main character.* She is a writer of mysteries who solves cases in her spare time. Each week she comes upon at least one murder victim. However, the actual murder isn't shown. Jessica figures out who committed the crime by asking questions of everyone. She goes over every detail dozens of times. Finally, she figures out the one thing the murderer forgot to cover up.

In this week's show, Ms. Fletcher visits an old friend in a small Southern town. A murder takes place while she is there. The people in the town are angry. A mob* forms. Tensions are high. It looks as if things are about to explode. Jessica solves the crime and exposes* the murderer, just before the angry mob tries to hang the suspect.* The suspect, she finds, was wrongly put in jail for the crime.

You may not know how to say all the words you read in the review. When this happens, think about other words you know that look like the new words. The new words may sound the same as the ones you know.

How It Works

In Lesson 1 you learned about the vowels: a, e, i, o, and u. You found out that you can say each vowel two ways. Think of the words *date* and *sand*. The *a* in *date* is a long vowel. It sounds like the letter *a* in the alphabet. The *a* in *sand* is a short vowel.

Have you ever seen the TV show "Murder, She Wrote"? It's a popular mystery show.

Now look at these pairs of words. The first vowel in each pair is the same. However, the vowel sounds in each pair are different.

fame	bat	grow	sock
equal	send	flute	sun
iron	chin		

Try It

Look at the underlined words in items 1 and 2 below. In some of these words, the *first vowel* is a long vowel. Write only these words in the answer blanks.

1. Some people <u>like</u> to watch mystery <u>shows</u> on television. Trying to <u>solve</u> the crime is <u>fun</u>.

_____ _____

The *o* in *shows* and the *i* in *like* are long vowels. The *o* in *solve* and the *u* in *fun* are short vowels.

2. The stories in "Murder, <u>She Wrote</u>" are never violent. They are <u>sometimes funny</u>. They are usually believable.

_____ _____

The *e* in *she* and the *o* in *wrote* are long vowel sounds. The *o* in *sometimes* and the *u* in *funny* are short vowel sounds.

Practice

Write each underlined word on one of the long answer blanks.
Look at the *first vowel* in the word. Write *long* on the short
answer blank if the word has a long vowel sound. Write *short* on
the short answer blank if the vowel has a short vowel sound.

1. On television, you can see live shows with jazz
   performers.

   _____ _____   _____ _____

   _____ _____

2. You can hear a discussion of current events.

   _____ _____   _____ _____

   _____ _____

3. Some people watch adventure movies, while others enjoy
   old movies from the 1940s and the 1950s.

   _____ _____   _____ _____

   _____ _____

4. Reviewers write their opinions of TV shows in
   newspapers and magazines.

   _____ _____   _____ _____

   _____ _____

5. Reviewers write about the quality of the acting and about
   the stories.

   _____ _____   _____ _____

   _____ _____

Check your answers on page 118.

"Wheel of Fortune" is one of the most popular TV game shows ever.

Follow-Up

Write the name of your favorite TV show. Then write some words that describe it. For example:

"Wheel of Fortune"

fast-paced

makes you think

entertaining

a game of luck and intelligence

two players

many blanks that need
  to be filled in with letters

the winner is the person who
  correctly guesses the words

Now write a short review of the TV show. Write from five to ten sentences. Describe the show so that someone who has never seen it will know what it is like.

Music

What You Know   Imagine for a moment that you live in New York City. It is summer, and this weekend a West-African rock musician is giving an outdoor concert. His name is Ali Farka Touré (AH-lee FAHR-kah TOOR-ay). Assume that you have never heard of him. You have never even heard African rock music. Lucky for you, there is a review in the newspaper. You decide to read it. It may help you decide whether or not to buy a ticket for the concert. Here is what the review says:

> Tonight West-African rock will be performed by Ali Farka Touré. Mr. Touré's sound is slow and easy, as if time were on his side. His guitar playing is excellent. His singing is soulful. He is a singer who sometimes gives advice, such as "Don't turn your back on your people when they need you." His music sounds like John Lee Hooker's—and it's every bit as good. Mr. Touré and his band can play fast, or they can play slowly. His musical abilities seem limitless. He is *that* good!

Based on this review, do you think that you would buy tickets to see Ali Farka Touré? The review states that Mr. Touré's music is *soulful* and that his abilities seem *limitless*. The word endings *ful* and *less* on the words *soul* and *limit* might make the difference as to whether or not you decide to go to the concert.

Ali Farka Touré plays West African rock music.

25

How It Works

Several of the words in the music review end in **suffixes** (SUF-ihk-sihz). A suffix is one or more letters added to the end of a word. A suffix changes the meaning of the word it is added to.

Here are four words from the review that end in suffixes:

soul**ful**   sing**er**   limit**less**   slow**ly**

The suffix *ful* means "full of."

Mr. Touré's singing is *soulful*. (His singing is full of soul.)

The suffix *er* added to a word can show that the word names a person who does something.

He is a *singer* who sometimes gives advice, such as "Don't turn your back on your people when they need you." (A singer is a person who sings.)

The suffix *less* means "without."

His musical abilities seem *limitless*. (His musical abilities are without limit.)

The suffix *ly* means "in a certain way."

Mr. Touré and his band can play up-tempo* or *slowly*. (He and his band can play in a slow way.)

Try It

Read the sentences below. Circle the suffix of each underlined word. Then put a check mark next to the correct meaning of the suffix.

1. Everyone was <u>hopeful</u> that the concert would begin on time.

_____ person

_____ full of

_____ without

The *ful* ending means "full of." The people were full of hope.

2. The <u>drummer</u> played a fast, pounding beat.

_____ person

_____ full of

_____ without

The *er* ending shows that you are talking about a person—
a person who is playing the drums.

3. One song was about a <u>penniless</u> person.

_____ person

_____ full of

_____ without

The *less* ending means "without." The song, then, was
about a person without any pennies, or in other words,
without money.

What makes a musical group popular? Is it the words they sing, the music they
play, or the way they perform on stage?

Practice

Read the sentences below. Look at the underlined words. Choose the suffix that best fits the meaning. Write the suffix in the space provided on the underline.

1. Some perform＿＿＿s enjoy playing outdoors.

    ly   er   ful   less

2. They are thank＿＿＿ when the weather is good.

    ly   er   ful   less

3. On the other hand, some musicians are fear＿＿＿ of huge crowds.

    ly   er   ful   less

4. They would rather play calm＿＿＿ in a quiet setting.

    ly   er   ful   less

5. Some musicians sing sad songs about hope＿＿＿ people.

    ly   er   ful   less

6. Others sing loud＿＿＿ about the great things life has to offer everyone.

    ly   er   ful   less

Check your answers on page 118.

Follow-Up

What musician or band would you like to see perform in a concert? Write a paragraph explaining why you would make this choice.

Movies

What You Know Have you ever heard of Sylvester Stallone? If so, can you name the movie he starred in in 1976? If not, you may be too young to remember *Rocky*. That movie was one of the most popular movies of the year—and of many years to follow.

Suppose *Rocky* comes to a theater in your town. Would you to go to see it? Do you know what it's about? Here's a short review. Read it. Then decide whether or not it's a movie you'd like to see.

Rocky—He's All Heart

Rocky is a 30-year-old boxer who never made it big. He's poor. He has nothing. People laugh when they hear the name he uses in the ring—the Italian Stallion. This guy isn't much of a fighting horse, they feel.

The world heavyweight boxing champion is Apollo Creed. Creed has decided to give an unknown fighter a chance to become the champion. So, guess who he picks to fight? Rocky, of course.

Sylvester Stallone, playing the part of Rocky, wins the heart of the audience. He's a big, tough guy who doesn't want to hurt anyone. He's a loner who stays to himself. He tells his troubles to his pet turtles. But he's got burning energy inside. His sad brown eyes and hurt-looking mouth make him sympathetic. People are on his side. Everyone wants him to win. At times during the movie, the cheers for Rocky are so loud that it's difficult to hear what's going on.

Go directly to the movies to see *Rocky* if you want to spend time with a real winner.

Are there any words in the review that you have never seen before? If so, there are a few ways to find out what they mean. You can look up a word in a dictionary. Also, you can guess the meaning of a word by figuring out the meaning of the words and sentences near the word.

Sylvester Stallone appeared in the box office hit *Rocky*.

How It Works

Perhaps you don't know what *stallion* or *loner* or *sympathetic* means.

In the review, you learn that Rocky is called the *Italian Stallion*. A *stallion* (STAL-yuhn) is a male horse. You may have been able to figure that out by reading the words in the next sentence in the review: *This guy isn't much of a fighting horse, they feel.*

Do you know what the word *loner* means? Here's how to figure it out.

1. Look at the words that follow *loner* in the sentence. They tell you that he stays to himself. These words tell you that a *loner* is someone who is alone.

2. Look at the sentence that follows the one in which *loner* appears. *He tells his troubles to his pet turtles.* The fact that he tells his troubles to his pet turtles and not to a friend, wife, or relative gives you another clue that a *loner* is someone who stays alone.

How about the word *sympathetic*? Do you know what it means? By looking at the other words in the sentence in which the word *sympathetic* appears, and by looking at the sentence that follows it, you can make a good guess. Sad eyes and a hurt-looking mouth cause everybody to be on his side. Everyone wants him to win. People like him. A sympathetic person is someone other people feel kindly toward.

Rocky was so popular that another Rocky movie, called *Rocky II*, was made.

Try It

Read the sentences below. Then guess what the word *hostile* means. To do this, first look at the words near the word you don't know. Also look at the sentences near the new word. Then take a good guess.

> In the movie, Rocky meets a kind girl in a pet store. Even though many people say *hostile* things about him, she always says nice things to him.

What does *hostile* mean? Write your answer on the blank.

_____

Hostile means "unfriendly." The first sentence tells you that the girl is *kind*. The second tells you that she always says nice things. The words *even though* tell you that something is the opposite of something else. Therefore, *hostile* is the opposite of *nice*. So you can guess that *hostile* means not nice, or unfriendly.

Practice

Read the sentences below. Then figure out what the underlined word in each sentence means. Write the meaning of this word on the answer blank.

1. In the early 1900s, Hollywood, California, was the center of the movie-making industry. Its <u>ideal</u> climate made it easy to shoot movies outdoors. It didn't rain too much. The weather never got too cold or too hot.

What does <u>ideal</u> mean?

_____

2. Most actors do not perform <u>death-defying</u> actions, like falling out of planes and jumping from moving trains. They leave the more dangerous moves to people who are trained in this kind of thing.

What does <u>death-defying</u> mean?

_____

Check your answers on page 118.

Follow-Up

Look through a newspaper or magazine and find a movie review. Bring it to class. Students can discuss these reviews as a class or in pairs or groups. Then write your own review of your favorite movie.

Books

What You Know When people look for a good book to read, how do they find one? They may ask a friend to suggest a favorite. They may look on the bookstore shelves and pick out a book by its cover. Maybe they read the first paragraph of a book to see whether it "sounds" good.

Another way to find a good book is to read a book review. Book reviews are in newspapers and magazines.

Read this book review. Based on what it says, do you think you would want to read the book ?

Invisible Man

Several movies have been done about invisible men. In those movies, people became invisible by some accident of science. In Ralph Ellison's book, *Invisible Man*, the main character is born invisible—he is born an African American.

The main character, whose name is never given, is born in the South, attends college at a southern university, and then moves to Harlem, a well-known African American community in New York City. The main character tells the story, and so the reader is able to see everything that happens through his eyes. As he meets and gets to know all different kinds of people—African Americans and white people, good people and bad, racists and nonracists of both races—he comes to understand himself.

As the book begins, he feels that he is invisible. Because he is black, white people don't "see" him. They look past him or through him as if he were really invisible. He also feels that he is blind, since he cannot see, or understand, what happens to him.

At the end of the book, he comes to understand that he is neither blind nor invisible. It is the blindness of others that prevents them from seeing him.

Although this book was written in the early 1950s, it is as true, meaningful, and important a work now as it was 40 years ago.

Did you find any information in this review of special interest to you? Which of the details caught your attention? Based on the information in this review, do you think you would like to read this book?

Even though *Invisible Man* is fiction, it is a story about someone's life and experiences. If you like these kinds of books, you would probably enjoy reading *Invisible Man*. However, if you like reading biographies or mysteries, would *Invisible Man* be a good choice for you?

How It Works

Details in the book review give information that can help you decide whether or not to read *Invisible Man*. The details answer questions such as *who, what, where, when, why,* and *how.*

Sometimes people read just for fun. At other times, they read to learn something. When you read a book review, for example, you are reading to find out about a specific book.

You might ask, "*What* kind of book is this?" If it's a mystery and you don't like them, you might not want to read it.

You might also want to know *what* the book is about. *Invisible Man* is about a young African American man's life experiences. Do you like reading books about this?

Another question you might ask yourself as you read the review is, "*Who* is the author?" If you have enjoyed other books by this author, you might want to read this one too.

Suppose you like reading books that take place in 18th century England. By asking, "*Where* and *when* does this book take place?" you will find that *Invisible Man* is not for you.

This is a picture of a street in Harlem in New York City in the 1950s. This shows the way it looked when the Invisible Man lived there.

You also need to think about *how* a book might make you feel. Some books might make you feel afraid. Others might make you feel sad or angry. Some people enjoy reading books that make them have these feelings. Others don't.

Finally, you might ask, "*Why* would I want to read a book?" Is it about something you care about or are interested in? Maybe it's about something that you can relate to in your own life.

Try It

Read the following sentences. Then look back at the review on page 33 to help you answer the questions. Write your answers on the blank lines.

1. *Where* does *Invisible Man* take place? Does the whole book take place in one part of the country?

   _____

   Invisible Man starts in the South, and then it takes place in Harlem in New York City.

2. *Why* does the Invisible Man feel that he is invisible?

   _____

   The Invisible Man feels invisible because white people look through him, as if he is not there.

3. *When* was the book written? _____

   The book was written in the early 1950s.

4. *What* does the Invisible Man feel about being invisible at the end of the book?

   _____

   At the end of the book, the Invisible Man feels that people don't see him because they are blind. He no longer feels that he is invisible.

Practice

Read these sentences. Then answer the questions.

A great mystery book went on sale on August 20. It's called *From Potter's Field*. It's about a murder that takes place in Central Park in New York City. The book is fast-paced and well-written. There's lots of suspense* and action.

The author of the book, Patricia D. Cornwell believes that all the details in her books should be as real as possible. She uses real street names. She uses the names of real cities and towns.

1. Where does the murder take place?

_____

2. Who is the author?

_____

3. What does the author believe about the details of her books?

_____

Check your answers on page 118.

Follow-Up

Write a paragraph telling how you think *Invisible Man* would make you feel and why you would or wouldn't want to read it. Then find a book review about another book in a newspaper or magazine. After you finish reading the review, ask yourself, "What is it about? Where does it take place? Who is the main character? Where does the action in the book happen? How do you think you would feel when you read the book? Why do you or don't you want to read it?" Write one sentence that answers each question.

Photography

What You Know Do you ever look at old photographs of friends and family? If so, you may enjoy looking at them because they make a moment in time stand still. No matter what happens to the people in the picture, the picture will always stay the same. Nothing can change the look on the people's faces or the setting where the photograph was taken.

Some photographers become famous. The faces and places in their photographs have such a strong effect on us that they remain forever in our minds. One such photographer is Dorothea Lange.

Imagine that her photographs are being shown in an exhibit in your town. Do you think that you would want to see them based on this review?

Dorothea Lange's photographs can make you cry. Some of her photographs are of migrant workers in California. *Migrant* (MEYE-gruhnt) *workers* are farm workers who move from place to place to harvest crops. Most of them work under terrible conditions. They are paid very little. They work long hours. They are unhappy. The sad look on their faces shows that their lives are not easy.

Other photographs by Lange show Japanese Americans in California during World War II. These people are in "camps," where they were forced to stay by the U.S. government. The government felt that they were safer there, because the United States was at war with Japan. The people's faces show their sorrow.

Most of Lange's work shows poor people. The rich don't seem to interest her. After seeing Lange's work, you will walk away with strong feelings of having spent time with lonely people who are struggling hard to make a decent life. These realistic photographs will stay in your mind for a long time.

Perhaps not everyone would enjoy seeing Lange's photographs. For example, if you like to see people living an *easy* life, not a *hard* life, you might not want to see the show. If you don't like seeing *sad, unhappy* people, you also might not like the show.

The words *sad* and *unhappy* are synonyms. The words *easy* and *hard* are antonyms.

Dorothea Lange is one of the most respected photographers in American history.

How It Works

As you learned in Lesson 4, two words that mean the same are **synonyms**. Here are some examples:

rich   wealthy

happy   joyful

Two words that have opposite meanings are **antonyms**. Here are some examples:

day   night

neat   messy

Dorothea Lange's photographs are admired by people all over the world. Read these sentences about her work. Look at the underlined words.

1. Lange shows the <u>sad</u> faces of young people.

2. Lange shows the <u>joyless</u> faces of young people.

3. The <u>happy</u> faces of young people are rarely seen in Lange's photographs.

Sentence 1 contains the word *sad*. Sentence 2 uses the word *joyless* instead of *sad*. *Joyless* is a synonym for *sad*. Sentence 3 says that happy faces aren't seen very often. *Happy* is an antonym for *sad*. It means the opposite of *sad*.

38

Try It

The faces in Dorothea Lange's photographs stay with you a long time.

Read these sentences. Look carefully at the underlined word in the first sentence. Write the answer to the questions on the answer blanks.

1. Lange is <u>famous</u> for her portraits of farm workers.

2. Lange is well-known for her portraits of farm workers.

3. Lange may be unknown in certain parts of the world.

What word is a synonym for the word *famous?* _____

Well-known is a synonym for *famous. Well-known* means the same thing as *famous.*

Which word is an antonym for *famous?* _____

Unknown is an antonym for *famous. Unknown* is the opposite of *famous.*

Practice

Read the following sentences and look at the underlined words. Then answer the questions.

1. Lange shows many <u>poor</u> people. These penniless people live hard lives. Few, if any, ever become rich.

   a. Which word is a synonym for <u>poor</u>? _____

   b. Which word is an antonym for <u>poor</u>? _____

2. In the late 1930s and 1940s, there was not <u>a lot</u> of work for farm workers. There was, however, plenty of time for long conversations at the side of the road. The little work there was barely kept the workers busy.

   a. Which word is a synonym for <u>a lot</u>? _____

   b. Which word is an antonym for <u>a lot</u>? _____

3. It's easy to <u>remember</u> the faces in Lange's photographs. You can recall them without any trouble. The faces of people are so strong you can't easily forget them.

   a. Which word is a synonym for <u>remember</u>?

      _____

   b. Which word is an antonym for <u>remember</u>?

      _____

Check your answers on page 118.

Follow-Up

If you have any photograph albums, take a look through them. Make a list of synonyms and antonyms describing the way people and places look.

Unit
3

Fiction

Who's Telling the Story?

What You Know Have you ever heard anyone say, "Never pick up a hitchhiker*"? Why do you think people say this?

Read this paragraph from the story "The Hitchhiker," by Roald Dahl. Look closely at the details in the paragraph. Can you tell how the person telling the story feels about hitchhiking?

> Ahead of me I saw a man thumbing* a lift.* I touched the brake and brought the car to a stop beside him. I always stop for hitchhikers. I knew just how it used to feel to be standing on the side of a country road watching the cars go by. I hated the drivers for pretending they didn't see me, especially the ones in big cars with three empty seats.

In every story, someone has to tell what happens. The person telling the story tells it from his or her **point of view**. This means that the storyteller tells it the way he or she sees it. If the storyteller is one of the people in the story, the story is told from the storyteller's point of view. For example, in the paragraph above, the storyteller refers to himself or herself as "I" or "me." A story told in this way is told from a **first-person** point of view.

Stories can also be told from the **third-person** point of view. In this case, the storyteller is not a character in the story.

With the third-person point of view, the storyteller can see and know everything that is going on, not just how one person sees things or feels about things. The storyteller refers to the characters as "he," "she," or "they," or by their names. Here is the same paragraph, but this time it is told from the third-person point of view.

> Ahead of him he saw a man thumbing a lift. He touched the brake and brought the car to a stop beside him. He always stops for hitchhikers. He knew just how it used to feel to be standing on the side of the road watching the cars go by. He hated the drivers pretending they didn't see him, especially the ones in big cars with three empty seats.

Although the main details in the paragraph haven't changed, the storyteller has. This time, the story is told from a third-person point of view. The storyteller knows what the man in the story is thinking and feeling.

How It Works

In Lesson 9 you looked for facts in a book review. In this lesson you will look for facts in a work of fiction. A work of **fiction** (FIHK-shuhn) is a book or story that is made up from the writer's imagination. In the example about the hitchhiker, there are many details that give the storyteller's views about hitchhiking. To find these details, you can use the same steps here that you used in Lesson 9.

Think about what you need to know. Next ask yourself a question that starts with words such as *who*, *what*, *where*, *when*, *why*, or *how*.

Then look for the answer to that question in what you are reading. The answer can often be found in a single word or a few words. The answer may be a place, a date, a number, a person, or a fact.

Try It

Read this section from "The Hitchhiker" and answer the questions that follow. Read the hints above in How It Works as you answer the questions. Write your answers on the answer blanks.

He was a small ratty-faced* man with gray teeth. His eyes were dark and quick and clever, like rat's eyes, and his ears were slightly pointed at the top. He had a cloth cap on his head and he was wearing a grayish-colored jacket with enormous* pockets. The gray jacket, together with the quick eyes and the pointed ears, made him look more than anything like some sort of a huge human rat.

Would you pick up a hitchhiker?

Look back at the paragraph on page 43 to help you answer these questions.

1. What is the color of the jacket the hitchhiker is wearing?

_____

_____

The hitchhiker is wearing a grayish jacket. (The question starts with *what*. The answer is a color.)

2. *Where* was the cloth cap?

_____

_____

The cloth cap was on his head. (The question starts with *where*. The answer is a place.)

3. Why does the hitchhiker look like a rat?

_____

_____

He looks like a rat because of his gray jacket, quick eyes, and pointed ears. Rats are gray and have quick eyes and pointed ears. (The question starts with *why*. The answer will include one or more reasons.)

Now read this sentence and answer the questions.

I was driving up to London by myself. It was a lovely June day.

1. *Where* was he going? _____

He was going to London. (The question starts with *where*. The answer is a place.)

2. *Who* was he traveling with? _____

He was traveling alone, or with no one. (The question starts with *who*. The answer is a person or, in this case, a "nonperson,"—no one.)

Practice

Here is a paragraph from *The Adventures of Huckleberry Finn* by Mark Twain. Read this paragraph and then answer the questions that follow.

> That night after dinner, Miss Watson, the widow's skinny old sister, started pecking* at me. She told me all about the bad place where some people go after they die. I said I wished I was there. She got mad then, but I didn't mean no harm. All I wanted was a change.

1. To answer the question *who*, tell whether the paragraph is written from the first-person or third-person point of view.

   _____

2. Where did Miss Watson say some people go after they die?

   _____

3. Why did the storyteller say he wished he was there?

   _____

4. How did Miss Watson feel when he said he wished he was there?

   _____

5. When did Miss Watson start pecking at the storyteller?

   _____

6. What was Miss Watson's relationship to the widow?

   _____

Check your answers on page 118.

Follow-Up

Write a paragraph telling about something that happened between you and someone you know. Write it from your point of view (first person). Then rewrite it from the third-person point of view. Remember that this means that you know how the other person was thinking and feeling.

People (Characters)

What You Know Do you like a good story? Most people do. Some people like stories about war. Others like stories about poor people who get rich. Still others enjoy stories about detectives who solve crimes.

For some people, the most interesting part of any story is the people, or characters, in it. A character may be a mean, selfish old man or a shy, kind young woman. There could be a heartless gang member or a strong young boy. In a good story, you are on the side of the good guys and you hope that the bad guys get what they deserve.

One writer who has won many awards for his bestselling books is Tony Hillerman. He often writes about Native Americans. Usually, there's a murder or two that Officer Jim Chee and Lieutenant Joe Leaphorn have to solve.

Read this paragraph from Hillerman's book *Sacred Clowns.*

> "Look," he [Chee] said. "See those three boys almost directly across the plaza? Behind the women. Notice the one in the red shirt."
>
> "Yeah," Janet said. "It looks like him. But isn't he too tall?"
>
> "The description said five foot eight," Chee said. "That's pretty tall for a Pueblo* kid."

There are a few facts in this passage. One is that a person is wearing a red shirt. Another is that the boy the characters are looking for is supposed to be 5 feet 8 inches in height.

How It Works

Facts can be proven to be real or true. They do not change. You can count, measure, or see facts.

Opinions cannot be proven to be true. They are based on values. One way you can tell that a statement expresses a value is by looking for key words such as *good, bad, best, worst, easy, hard,* and *should.*

The following two sentences show an example of opinions based on values.

His shirt is the *best*-looking shirt of anyone's.

This will be the *easiest* case we've ever had.

Opinions may also be based on feelings or beliefs. Such opinions often start with *I think . . ., I feel . . .,* or *I believe. . . .*

I *think* we'll find him by noon.

I *believe* he's the one who committed the murder.

There can be many different opinions about the same thing.

Officer Chee is certain he will solve the crime.

His partner isn't so sure.

Tony Hillerman is a bestselling author of many books about Native Americans. He writes about Navajo [NAHV-uh-hoh] police officers. The Navajo people are Native Americans who live in the states of Arizona, New Mexico, and Utah.

Try It

Write F in the answer blank if the sentence is a fact. Write O if the sentence is an opinion.

___ **1.** Blizzard was wearing his Bureau of Indian Affairs uniform with a baseball cap.

Fact. The statement can be proven by looking at Blizzard's clothing.

___ **2.** He was talking slowly.

Opinion. Some people might think that he was talking slowly. Others might think that he is talking normally or quickly.

___ **3.** Jim Chee was reading a book of short stories by a favorite writer of his.

Fact. It can be proven by looking at the book.

___ **4.** Blizzard was the best-dressed man in the room.

Opinion. Some people might think that he was well-dressed. Others might not.

___ **5.** Leaphorn was 30 minutes late for the meeting.

Fact. The statement can be proven by looking at a clock and in an appointment book.

___ **6.** Lieutenant Leaphorn is the best detective in the Navajo Tribal Police.

Opinion. Some people may believe that he is the best detective. Others may disagree.

___ **7.** Applebee was shot three times in the chest with a forty-five.

Fact. It is something that can be proven when the police find out what took place.

Practice

Read the following sentences. Write F in the answer blank if the sentence is a fact. Write O if the sentence is an opinion.

_____ **1.** Tony Hillerman was once president of the Mystery Writers of America.

_____ **2.** He has received the Edgar and Grand Masters Awards.

_____ **3.** His characters are the most interesting characters in mystery novels.

_____ **4.** Hillerman has written *Coyote Waits*, *Talking God*, and *A Thief in Time*, among other books.

_____ **5.** Hillerman's best book is *Dance Hall of the Dead*.

_____ **6.** In Hillerman's books, Officer Jim Chee and Lieutenant Joe Leaphorn are part of the Navajo Tribal Police.

_____ **7.** A bullet kills Officer Jim Chee's friend Del in the novel *Coyote Waits*.

_____ **8.** Del was one of the nicest guys a person could know.

_____ **9.** Nobody writes a better suspense* novel than Tony Hillerman.

_____ **10.** Leaphorn and Chee solve the hardest cases.

Check your answers on page 119.

Follow-Up

Talk to people who enjoy reading suspense novels. Ask them why they like to read that kind of book. Then write a short paragraph about what they tell you.

What Happens (Plot)

What You Know   Suppose that you have seen a movie on TV that you really liked. You want to tell your friends about it the next day. Here is a group of sentences that are examples of what you might say about the movie:

Someone has put a bomb on a bus.

If the bus goes below 50 miles per hour, the bomb will explode.

If people try to get off the bus, the bomb will explode.

A police officer gets on the bus to try to help the passengers.

The bomber will blow up the bus if he doesn't get a lot of money.

What you describe with sentences like this is the plot of the movie. The **plot** of a movie or book is the story of the events and the order in which the events take place.

How It Works

Look again at the sentences above. What is the main idea? To find the **main idea** follow these steps:

1. Decide in a general way *what* or *who* all the sentences are about. This is called the **topic**.

2. Find the most important and the most general point that is made.

3. Look at the other sentences. They contain the details that support or help explain the main idea.

The main idea is item 1: *Someone has put a bomb on a bus*. All the other sentences support this idea.
Here is part of a story called "Everything Stuck to Him," by Raymond Carver.

You're going to have to choose, the girl said. Carl or us. I mean it.

What do you mean? The boy said.

You heard what I said, the girl said. If you want a family, you're going to have to choose.

They stared at each other. Then the boy took up his hunting gear and went outside. He started the car. He went around to the car windows and, making a job of it, scraped away the ice.

He turned off the motor and sat a while. And then he got up out and went back inside.

This is what took place:

1. A girl tells a boy he has to choose between Carl and his family.

2. The two stare at each other.

3. The boy picks up his hunting gear and goes outside.

4. He starts the car.

5. He scrapes ice off the windows.

6. He turns off the motor and sits a while.

7. He goes back inside.

What is the main idea? The main idea is in item 1: *the boy has to choose between Carl and his family*. This is the most important point. All the other sentences support this point about his making this decision: he goes outside, he thinks about what to do as he starts the car, he scrapes ice off the window and sits a while, and then he goes back inside.

Raymond Carver (1938–1988) wrote many poems and short stories.

Try It

Read the sentences below, from the same short story by Raymond Carver, "Everything Stuck to Him." Then put a check mark next to the sentence that contains the main idea.

> She watched while he laid out his things. Hunting coat, shell bag, boots, socks, hunting cap, long underwear, pump gun.
> What time will you be back? the girl said.

_____ The girl is annoyed.

_____ The boy enjoys getting dressed.

_____ The boy is going hunting.

_____ The boy likes to lay out his clothing.

_____ The girl wishes that she could go hunting too.

The main idea is that the boy is going hunting. The other sentences are details that support this: He lays out all his hunting things. The girl asks what time he will return. These sentences are about the boy leaving to go hunting.

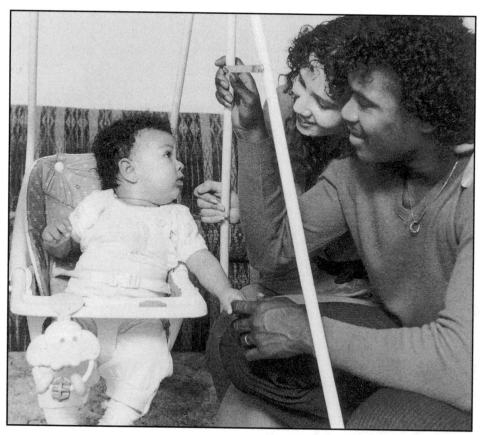

Babies need a lot of love and attention. Parents need a lot of patience.

Practice

Read this passage from "Everything Stuck to Him." Then put a check mark next to the main idea in the group of sentences that follows.

It was the baby's cries that woke him up.

The light was on out there, and the girl was standing next to the crib rocking the baby in her arms. She put the baby down, turned out the light, and came back to bed.

He heard the baby cry. This time the girl stayed where she was. The baby cried fitfully* and stopped. The boy listened, then dozed.* But the baby's cries woke him again. The living room light was burning. He sat up and turned on the lamp.

I don't know what's wrong, the girl said, walking back and forth with the baby. I've changed and fed her, but she keeps on crying. I'm so tired I'm afraid I might drop her. . . .

It was a quarter to four, which gave him forty-five minutes. He crawled into bed and dropped off. But a few minutes later the baby was crying again, and this time they both got up.

The boy did a terrible thing. He swore.

For God's sake, what's the matter with you? the girl said to the boy. Maybe she's sick or something. Maybe we shouldn't have given her the bath.

The main idea is:

_____ The parents couldn't sleep.

_____ Maybe the baby is sick.

_____ The girl doesn't know what's wrong.

_____ The boy had only 45 minutes to sleep.

_____ The baby cried and woke up the parents.

Check your answers on page 119.

Follow-Up

Write a list giving reasons why you think that the baby is crying in the above paragraphs. Then write one sentence that is the main idea of the list.

Place (Setting)

What You Know   Right now, you are probably in a room—perhaps in a school. Most likely, you walked to the school, walked into the room, found a chair, sat down, opened your book, and began reading. It was easy to do these things. The room, with desks and chairs, provides a place, or **setting**, for you to do your work.

Do you think that you could accomplish the same things if —right this second—you found yourself in another setting? Imagine that you are now on a large, beautiful cruise ship sailing on the ocean, or in an unheated cabin up north where the temperature is 25 degrees below zero. Do you think that you could do the same things you are doing now? Probably not. The setting, or place, affects what you do and how you feel.

Read this short passage from "A Trip for Mrs. Taylor." As you read, think about the series of steps she takes to accomplish her goal. Does the setting help Mrs. Taylor do what she has to do?

> Mrs. Taylor got out of bed at five o'clock that morning. This was an hour ahead of her usual time. She moved around her attic* room quietly, making herself her morning cup of tea on the hot plate. She dressed so as not to disturb her landlady, Mrs. Connell, on the floor below.

Mrs. Taylor lives in an attic, one floor above her landlady. It appears that Mrs. Taylor is getting ready for her day. To accomplish that, she does several things in her room:

1. She gets out of bed.

2. She moves around the room quietly.

3. She makes herself a cup of tea.

4. She gets dressed.

How It Works

In order to accomplish a goal, you should follow some simple steps.

First decide what your goal is. Suppose that your goal is to study for the GED tests.

Next think of some things you need to do. For example, set aside some time, get your books, go to a library or to school (or wherever you plan to study), sit in a classroom or library, and start studying.

Finally, decide what to do first, second, and so on. For example:

1. Set aside time.

2. Get your books.

3. Go to school.

4. Go into a classroom.

5. Find a place to sit.

6. Sit down.

7. Open a book.

8. Start reading.

Here is more information about Mrs. Taylor. As you read, think about what she does to get ready for her day.

After she had drunk her tea and eaten a slice of toast, she washed her cup and saucer in some water she had gotten from the bathroom the evening before. She then put them away on her "kitchen" shelf in the clothes closet. She tiptoed down the steep stairs to the bathroom and washed her face and hands.

Mrs. Taylor did some tasks in order. She decided what she wanted to do first, second, and so on.

1. She drank her tea and ate a slice of toast.

2. She washed her cup and saucer.

3. She put away the cup and saucer.

4. She tiptoed down the steep steps.

5. She walked into the bathroom.

6. She washed her face and hands.

Try It

In this passage, which takes place late at night on a quiet street, a woman has an important goal. As you read, think of what the goal is and how she achieves it.

> She was a large woman with a large purse that had everything in it but hammer and nails. It had a long strap and she carried it slung across her shoulder. It was about eleven o'clock at night, and she was walking alone, when a boy ran up behind her and tried to snatch her purse. The strap broke with the single tug the boy gave it from behind. But the boy's weight, and the weight of the purse combined caused him to lose his balance so, instead of taking off full blast as he had hoped, the boy fell on his back on the sidewalk, and his legs flew up. The large woman simply turned around and kicked him right square in his blue-jeaned sitter. Then she reached down, picked the boy up by his shirt front, and shook him until his teeth rattled.

The woman's goal was to catch the thief. This is how she did it. Arrange the actions in the order in which they took place.

_____ She picked up the boy by his shirt.

_____ She reached down.

_____ She turned around and kicked the boy.

_____ She shook the boy.

If you numbered the actions 3, 2, 1, 4, you were correct.

What would you do if someone stole something of yours—and it was almost midnight and you were on a deserted street?

Practice

What steps would you take to keep these ants from getting on you?

The person in this passage is trying to keep millions of ants from eating him alive. After you read the passage, number the steps he takes in the order in which they took place.

> He pulled on high leather boots and put on heavy gloves. He stuffed the spaces between pants and boots, gloves and arms, shirt and neck, with gasoline-soaked rags. With close-fitting goggles,* he shielded* his eyes. Finally, he plugged his nose and ears with cotton. The men poured gasoline over his clothes.

_____ Men poured gasoline over his clothes.

_____ He put on goggles.

_____ He pulled on his boots and gloves.

_____ He plugged his nose and ears with cotton.

_____ He stuffed the spaces between his boots and gloves with gasoline-soaked rags.

Check your answers on page 119.

Follow-Up

Write a list of the steps you have taken to achieve a goal. The goal might have been simply to leave the house on time, or it could have been to get a new job.

Tone

What You Know   When you listen to what people say and how they say things, you can sometimes tell how they feel. For example, suppose a person has just gone to the hospital. There are several ways to talk about this, for example:

> Jenny's sick. She just went to the hospital. I just visited her at the hospital.

In this case, the speaker's words are direct and matter-of-fact.

> Jennie's sick again—for the six-hundredth time! She's back at the hospital. It's like a second home to her. By this time she probably knows all the doctors by their first names.

Here the speaker is being sarcastic. *Being sarcastic* means saying sharp, cutting, unkind things, often to make fun of someone or to put someone down.

> Jenny's sick. I'm going to the hospital this minute to see whether I can do something for her or her family.

This speaker is concerned and sympathetic.

There are three tones expressed in these examples: direct, sarcastic, and concerned. **Tone** is the attitude of a speaker or writer toward the subject.

In the examples, something has happened: Jenny has gone to the hospital. The reason: she is sick.

How It Works

One thing often leads to another. *Why* something happens is the **cause**. For example, if someone gets very sick, this might *cause* the person to go to the hospital. *Getting sick* is *why* someone goes to the hospital.

The result of a cause is an **effect**—it is *what* happens. For example, getting sick causes someone to go to the hospital. *Going to the hospital* is the *effect* or result of getting sick. It is what happens.

Try It

Here are the first two sentences of a short story by Jerome Weidman called "My Father Sits in the Dark." The sentences state an *effect*.

> My father has a peculiar* habit. He is fond of* sitting in the dark, alone.

Read these sentences from the story. See whether you can figure out which group of sentences gives the *cause* of his father's sitting in the dark. Put a check mark next to the one you choose.

___ **1.** Perhaps he needs help. Why doesn't he speak? Why doesn't he frown or laugh or cry? Why doesn't he do something? Why does he just sit there?

___ **2.** "Well, what do you *think* about, Pa? Why do you just sit here? What's worrying you? What do you think about?"

___ **3.** "Why do you sit here so late in the dark?" "It's nice," he says. "I can't get used to the lights. We didn't have lights when I was a boy in Europe."

___ **4.** If only I knew what he thinks about. If I only knew that he thinks at all. I might not be able to help him. He might not even need help.

What causes the father to sit in the dark? The answer is number 3. The father sits in the dark because he can't get used to the lights. He never had lights when he was a boy. None of the other answers tells *why* the father sits in the dark.

The son wants to know why his father sits in the dark.

Practice

Read each sentence below. Then put a check mark next to the cause that leads to the effect.

1. Effect: He tiptoes into his room.

    Cause: _____ His mother is making dinner.

                   _____ He doesn't want to disturb his father.

                    _____ His father is at the movies.

2. Effect: A son asks his father why he sits in the dark.

    Cause: _____ The son is bored.

                    _____ The son is angry.

                    _____ The son is curious.

3. Effect: The son turns out the light.

    Cause: _____ The father doesn't like the light.

                    _____ The son likes a bright room.

                    _____ The light is needed in order to read.

Check your answers on page 119.

Follow-Up

Three different tones or attitudes are discussed in this lesson—direct, sarcastic, and sympathetic. Write a list of at least three other tones or attitudes that you know of.

Unit
4

Drama

Dialogue

What You Know   When you watch a comedy show on TV, you are watching the result of a **teleplay**, which is the written version of the show. The comedy show is a kind of drama. **Drama** (DRAH-muh) is a type of literature that is meant to be acted.

The kind of drama that has been around the longest is the play. A play is done live on a stage in a theater. The audience watches the actors on the stage.

Plays are divided into major parts called **acts**. An act may be broken down into smaller parts called **scenes**. People who write plays are called **playwrights** (PLAY-reyets). The written version of a play is called a **script**. Movies are also dramas. The written versions of movies are called **screenplays**.

The conversation, or the words people speak, in dramas is called **dialogue** (DEYE-uh-lawg). The sentences and paragraphs in dialogue are called **lines**.

Just as in speaking and in other forms of writing, some things that people say in plays are facts. Other things are opinions.

A play is meant to be performed live before an audience.

How It Works

In Lesson 12 you learned about facts and opinions. There are a few ways to tell the difference.

Facts can be proven to be real or true.

Miguel has been late to work six times this year.

This can be proven by checking a time card to see how many times Miguel has been late.

Opinions cannot be proven to be true. They are based on values. One way you can tell that a statement expresses a value is by looking for key words such as *good, bad, better, best, worst, easy, hard,* and *should.*

Jim is the best worker on the job.

Opinions may also be based on feelings or beliefs. Such opinions often start with *I think . . ., I feel . . .,* or *I believe. . . .*

I think that you are leaving because you are scared.

There can be more than one opinion about the same thing.

You're leaving because you're meeting someone else.

You're leaving because you don't love me anymore.

Try It

Read this short dialogue.

MAC:	I wrote you a few letters. Did you ever get them?
SUE ANNE:	No.
MAC:	Well, your mama didn't have to give them to you. Courts gave her complete jurisdiction.* Quite rightly, I guess, considering my state at the time.
SUE ANNE:	I told Mama I was coming here. She told me she'd have me arrested if I did. Then Harry reminded her that I'm eighteen now and I don't have to mind anybody.

Write F in the answer blank if the sentence is a fact. Write O if the sentence is an opinion.

____ **1.** Sue Anne is 18 years old.

Fact. This can be checked by looking at a birth certificate.

____ **2.** Mac is Sue Anne's father.

Fact. This can be proven by looking at birth records or having blood tests done.

____ **3.** Mac was not a good father.

Opinion. Many people, including a judge, may feel this way. Others might disagree.

____ **4.** Mac writes good letters.

Opinion. Whether or not a letter is well-written depends on a person's feelings.

____ **5.** The courts gave Sue Anne's mother care of her daughter.

Fact. The court records can be checked to find this out.

____ **6.** Mac is a bad person.

Opinion. This states a value.

The play being performed in the picture is called *Othello* (fact). It was written hundreds of years ago by William Shakespeare (fact). Many of his plays are performed all around the world today (fact). He was the greatest playwright that ever lived (opinion).

Practice

Read the following dialogue, in which the two characters are speaking about burying a dog.

KARL: Well, it's finished.

MARSHA: You didn't take long.

KARL: It wasn't a big hole. He wasn't a big dog.

MARSHA: You hardly stepped outside before you're back.

KARL: What did you want me to do—sing a hymn over him? The ground's hard this time of year.

MARSHA: The ground's not the only thing that's hard this time of year. You must've barely covered him.

KARL: You watched me from the window, didn't you? You saw how deep I dug—up to my knees.

MARSHA: I should've taken him to the animal hospital.

KARL: Too late for that now.

MARSHA: I mean to cremate* instead of letting you bury him!

KARL: Listen, don't blame yourself—or me. You think you should've taken him before, when he got sick. He was 17 years old. I miss him just as much as you do. He was old, that's all.

MARSHA: I feel old.

Write F in the answer blank if the sentence is a fact. Write O if the sentence is an opinion.

___ **1.** A dog has been buried.

___ **2.** The dog was not a big dog.

___ **3.** The two people are old.

___ **4.** The dog was 17 years old.

___ **5.** The two people didn't take the dog to the animal hospital.

Check your answers on page 120.

Follow-Up

Write a list of three ways in which watching a live play would be different from watching a movie.

People (Characters)

What You Know   **Characters** are the people in a play. Characters are very much like you and your friends—real people with real feelings doing real things. Could these sentences about one character be someone you know?

> She helps around the house with cooking and cleaning.
> She does good things for other people.
> She works part-time to help the family.
> She baby-sits in the neighborhood.
> She gives people nice gifts for their birthdays.

If these five sentences describe one of your friends, you have done a good job in choosing friends. The main idea of the group of sentences is that this person does good things for other people.

How It Works

In Lesson 13 you learned about finding the main idea in a group of sentences. To find the main idea, follow these steps:

1. First decide in a general way what all the sentences are about—the topic. Read the following sentences.

> Joel breaks promises he makes.
> Joel says he did things he did not do.
> Joel cheats on tests.
> Joel is a dishonest person.
> Joel does not pay back money he owes.

All the sentences are about Joel.

2. Now find the most important or the most general point that is made about Joel. It is *Joel is a dishonest person*. This is the main idea of all the sentences. Each of the other sentences has something to do with Joel and his dishonesty. These sentences contain the details that support, or help explain, the main idea.

Try It

Read these lines from a play called *True West* by Sam Shepard. The two characters, Lee and Austin, describe the "old lady," their mother.

LEE: I never realized the old lady was so security-minded.

AUSTIN: How do you mean?

LEE: Made a little tour this morning. She's got locks on everything. Locks and double-locks and chain locks and—What's she got that's so valuable?

AUSTIN: Antiques, I guess. I don't know.

LEE: Antiques? Brought everything with her from the old place, huh. Just the same crap we always had around. Plates and spoons.

AUSTIN: I guess they have personal value to her. . . . Well, it must mean something to her or she wouldn't save it.

Sam Shepard is a playwright and an actor.

Read the sentences below. Put a check mark next to the one that contains the main idea.

___ **1.** The mother is security-minded about the things in her home.

___ **2.** The mother values the things in her home.

___ **3.** The mother puts locks on the doors.

___ **4.** The mother puts double-locks and chains on the doors.

___ **5.** The boys think the objects in their mother's home is junk.

The main idea is in sentence 2: *The mother values the things in her home.* The other sentences support the main idea.

Here are some lines of dialogue from a play by Arthur Miller called *Death of a Salesman*. As you read, think about the character Willie and his attitude toward his neighborhood.

WILLY: The street is lined with cars. There's not a breath of fresh air in the neighborhood. The grass don't grow any more, you can't raise a carrot in the backyard. They should've had a law against apartment houses. Remember those two beautiful elm trees out there? When I and Biff hung the swing between them?

LINDA: Yeah, like being a million miles from the city.

WILLY: They should've arrested the builder for cutting those down. They massacred* the neighborhood. . . .

Read the lines below. Put a check mark next to the one that contains the main idea.

___ **1.** The grass don't grow any more.

___ **2.** You can't raise a carrot in the backyard.

___ **3.** They should've had a law against apartment houses.

___ **4.** They massacred the neighborhood.

___ **5.** Remember those two beautiful elm trees out there?

The main idea is in line 4: *They massacred the neighborhood.* The other sentences support the main idea.

In *Death of a Salesman*, Willie Loman often speaks about how things were better in the past.

Practice

Read these lines of dialogue from the play *A View from the Bridge*, by Arthur Miller. The character Eddie is speaking to his daughter Catherine about her boyfriend.

EDDIE: Catherine? *She turns to him.* I was just tellin' Beatrice . . . if you wanna go out, like . . . I mean I realize maybe I kept you home too much. Because he's the first guy you ever knew, y'know? I mean now that you got a job, you might meet some fellas, and you get a different idea, y'know? I mean you could always come back to him, you're still only kids, the both of yiz. What's the hurry? Maybe you'd get around a little bit, you grow up a little more, maybe you'll see different in a couple of months. I mean you be surprised, it don't have to be him.

Read the lines below. Put a check mark next to the one that contains the main idea.

_____ **1.** Maybe I kept you home too much.

_____ **2.** You might meet some fellas.

_____ **3.** Maybe you'd get around a little bit.

_____ **4.** I mean you be surprised, it don't have to be him.

_____ **5.** Because he's the first guy you ever knew, y'know?

Check your answers on page 120.

Follow-Up

Think of someone you know who might make an interesting character in a play. Write two or three lines of dialogue that this person might say.

What Happens (Plot)

What You Know   Have you ever had to quit a job? Why did you have to quit? Maybe you didn't get along with your boss. Maybe the job was getting in the way of your studying for the GED. Perhaps you had to quit in order to get a different, better job.

In a play by August Wilson called *Fences*, a character named Cory quits his job at the A&P. Cory's father, Troy, is upset. The reason Cory quits is so that he can play football. He's hoping to go to college on a football scholarship.

August Wilson won many awards for his play *Fences*.

How It Works

In Lesson 15 you learned about cause and effect. An event that makes something happen is a *cause*. This explains *why* something happened. The result of a cause is the *effect*. This is *what* happened.

You can use cause and effect to help you understand events in the plot of a play. As you learned in Lesson 13, the plot in a work of literature is the story of the events and the order of events that take place.

In the play *Fences*, one event is that Cory quits his job because he needs time to practice football. The cause is his need to have more time to practice football. The effect is that he quits his job.

Cause: Cory and his father have totally different values about almost everything.

Effect: _____ Cory and his father agree on most things.

_____ Cory and his father often disagree.

_____ Cory must leave home.

Cory and his father often disagree. When two people have different values, they do not see eye-to-eye on most things. Therefore, they often disagree.

Put a check mark next to the effect that resulted from the cause.

Cause: Troy does not have money for anything other than paying the rent and buying food and clothing.

Effect: _____ Troy cannot afford to buy his son the TV set that he wants.

_____ Troy can afford to buy a new car.

_____ Troy buys presents for all his relatives.

Troy cannot afford to buy his son the TV set that he wants. When people have money only for what is needed, they cannot buy things that are unnecessary to daily living. These things are considered "extras."

Try It

In the play *Fences*, a father and his son have different values. They often disagree.

Read the following sentence. Then put a check mark next to the effect that results from the cause.

Cause: For each of the past four years, a high school student has been voted the best football player in his state.

Effect: _____ The young man quits school.

_____ The young man is asked to attend a college on a football scholarship.

_____ The young man has to work at a low-paying job after he graduates from high school.

The young man is asked to attend a college on a football scholarship. If a student excels at a sport, people at a college are likely to offer the student a scholarship.

Practice

Read the following sentences. Then put a check mark next to the effect that results from the cause.

1. **Cause:** Cory wants more than anything else to go to college on a football scholarship.

    Effect: _____ He never practices football.

    _____ He quits school.

    _____ He practices football as much as he can.

2. **Cause:** Troy does not want his son to play football.

    Effect: _____ Troy tries to talk his son out of playing football.

    _____ Troy makes sure that his son has a football game to play in every evening.

    _____ Troy encourages his son to play football.

Check your answers on page 120.

Follow-Up

Very few people get to play professional sports. This is the effect. There may be more than one cause. Why do so few people play professional sports? Write down as many causes as you can.

Place (Setting)

What You Know Do you think that where you live makes a difference in your life? For example, would growing up on a farm in Iowa be like growing up in San Francisco? Do you think that growing up in a village in Mexico would be the same as growing up in Tokyo, Japan? Probably not.

The places mentioned above are similar in some ways and different in other ways. For example, life in big cities such as San Francisco and Tokyo may be similar.

Both cities may have a lot of noise and pollution. Both probably have many tall buildings, many people, and lots of crowded restaurants, movies, and museums. Both places probably have the latest in electronic equipment. People in both places are likely to dress in the latest clothing styles.

These cities differ greatly from towns or villages in the country. On a farm or in a village, there may not be any tall buildings. There may never be crowds. Most likely, there is little pollution. There may be few, if any, movies or museums. The latest in electronic equipment and in clothing styles may not have reached a farm or a village.

What similarities and differences do you see in these two places?

How It Works

Suppose that you are given the choice of living in two totally different places. You have to decide which is best for you.

First you **compare** the two places. This means that you look at what is the same about them. For example, both may be close to where you live now. Both may have good housing at a price you can afford. Both may have a job waiting for you. Both may have a beach nearby.

Then you **contrast** the two places. This means that you look at what is different about them. One is a big city, but the other is a small town. One place has a good public transportation system. However, the other does not.

After you compare and contrast the two places, you decide what to do.

Did you notice which kinds of words are used when you compare two things? Look for words such as *same*, *both*, *also*, and *too*.

Did you notice which kinds of words are used when you contrast two things? Look for words such as *but*, *however*, *even though*, and *although*.

Try It

The **setting** of a play is *where* (and *when*) the action takes place. Here is some information about the setting of two plays. Read the information. Then compare and contrast the two places. Put a check mark next to the right answer.

> The play takes place in the town of Crescent Grove, New Jersey. There's one grocery store, one drugstore, and one high school. Two traffic lights have recently been installed.

> The play takes place in southern Missouri, in a small town with one traffic light and several stores. There are many farms outside of town.

1. Both places are

_____ a. small towns.

_____ b. big cities.

_____ c. in Europe.

The correct answer is a. Both places are small towns. They are not big cities, because each has just a few stores. They are not in Europe, because the names of states in the United States are given.

2. A difference between the two places is that

_____ a. one place is in the United States, but the other is not.

_____ b. one place has a two traffic lights, and the other only has one.

_____ c. one place has a few stores, and the other has many large department stores.

The correct answer is b. The first place has two traffic lights; the second place has one.

This is a scene from a drama based on Charles Dickens' famous story *A Christmas Carol*. Are there any similarities between this setting and the place where you live? What are some differences?

UNIT 4   Drama

Practice

Here is some information about the setting of two plays. Read the information. Then compare and contrast the two places. Put a check mark next to the right answer.

The play takes place on the roof of a modern apartment building in New York City. It's 57 stories up. Many people are there, drinking and eating. It's a party.

The play takes place on the roof of a small run-down apartment building in Chicago. Two boys are trying to train pigeons to fly away and then come back to the roof. The roof is on top of a four-story, walk-up building.

1. Both settings are

_____ a. indoors, in a small, crowded room.

_____ b. outdoors, on a roof.

_____ c. in the Midwest.

2. One difference between the two settings is that

_____ a. one takes place in an apartment building, and the other takes place in a hotel.

_____ b. one takes place on the roof of a tall building, and the other takes place on the roof of a small building.

_____ c. both take place on the roofs of buildings.

Check your answers on page 120.

Follow Up

If you have a friend or relative who lives in a place that is very different from where you live, ask this person to tell you some of the good and bad things about living there. Write a paragraph comparing and contrasting both places. Then tell where you would rather be living and explain why.

Time (Setting)

What You Know   Imagine that you are watching a movie. In the first scene, you see several characters playing a game on a computer. They are wearing clothes similar to the ones you are wearing. From these details, you can make a good guess that the movie takes place in the present time.

Now suppose that you are watching a movie in which the people are riding in carriages pulled by horses through city streets. The women are wearing long dresses. You might guess that the movie takes place in the past, before cars were invented. Perhaps the movie takes place in the early 1900s.

Characters in movies don't have to say when an action occurs. By looking at the details, you know whether an action took place in the past or is taking place in the present.

By looking at the setting, you can make inferences about when the action is taking place.

How It Works

When you read, you will find that some information is not written in words. The same thing is true when you watch TV, a movie, or a play. Not all information is spoken or shown. You must **infer** (ihn-FUR) the information that is not given.

Making an inference (IHN-fuhr-uhns) means that you figure out what the unwritten information is. You do this by using the information that is written, together with what you know from your own life. You put these two things together to figure out what the unwritten information is. For example, if you see that the sun is just beginning to set, you can infer that it's evening.

When you make an inference, be careful not to infer more than you should.

In Lesson 19 you learned that the **setting** is *where* or *when* the action takes place. Read the following sentences that describe the setting of a play.

There's a small neat living room, with worn-looking furniture. Against a wall by a staircase is a TV set with a VCR on top of it. On the opposite wall, near a small window, is a wooden desk with a computer on top of it. The sofa is in the center of the room. To the left of the sofa is an end table, on top of which are a lamp, some papers, and a cordless phone.

Can you infer that it is the present time? (Yes. The VCR, computer, and cordless phone tell you that the time is very close to the present.)

Can you infer that the people who live there are poor? No. Even though the furniture is not in good condition, you do not have enough information to make this inference.

Try It

Read the following about the setting of a play.

An alley lined on both sides with small old brick apartment buildings is shown. All the buildings have fire escapes. Clotheslines hang between the buildings. The alley is dark. The bulb in a street lamp at the opening to the alley keeps going on and off. In the background, many apartment buildings can be seen. The buildings have television antennas on the roofs. A young man is seen coming down one of the fire escapes. He is carrying a small package under one arm. He looks down the street—out at the audience—as he comes down. The man is lightly dressed in a T-shirt and jeans.

Read the following inferences. Write yes on the blank line if you have enough information to make this inference. Write no if you do not.

_____ **1.** The scene takes place during winter.

No. There is nothing in the setting that suggests that it is winter. There is no snow or ice shown. The man is not wearing winter clothes, but only a T-shirt and jeans.

_____ **2.** The scene is set in the present.

No. Although it is possible that the scene is set in the present, you cannot be sure. Because of the television antennas, the scene must be set after televisions became fairly popular. This could be any time within the last 30 years.

_____ **3.** The alley is in a city.

Yes. The many small apartment buildings suggest that this alley is in the city rather than the country.

_____ **4.** It is night.

Yes. The alley is dark. Also, the street lamp is on. These things suggest that it is night.

Practice

First read the following information. Then read the sentences below. Write *yes* on the answer blank if you can make the inference. Write *no* if you cannot.

A man holding a big stick, similar to a baseball bat, is coming out of a huge opening on the side of a mountain, which is where he lives. He has a long beard and very long, messy hair. He is carrying a dead rabbit in his hand. A woman, who also has long, messy hair, walks by his side. They are wearing very few clothes, which are dirty. In the background, there are only rocks, trees, and bushes.

___ **1.** The man has killed the rabbit.

___ **2.** The two people have a hard life with few comforts.

___ **3.** The setting is a very long time ago, maybe many thousands of years ago.

___ **4.** The time of year is probably autumn.

___ **5.** The time of day is early morning.

Check your answers on page 120.

Follow-Up

Plan the opening scene of a play or movie that takes place in the 1960s. Write a list of what you would include to show it takes place in the 1960s rather than in any other period of time.

Unit
5

Poetry

Word Pictures (Imagery)

What You Know   Some people don't feel comfortable with poetry. Are you one of them? Is it because poetry seems difficult or strange? It doesn't have to. Do you know that poetry is all around you? The words to songs and raps are kinds of poems. Poems are in greeting cards and in TV ads. Children's nursery rhymes are also poems.

Poetry is the same as other kinds of writing because it expresses thoughts, ideas, and feelings. Poetry is different from other kinds of writing because in poems the sound of the words is important; sometimes the words rhyme. Also important is the rhythm (beat) of the words when they are said out loud.

Poetry is different from other kinds of writing in another way. Other kinds of writing have sentences and paragraphs. Even though poems have sentences, each line of a poem is important. A **line** of poetry is what it sounds like—a group of words that are all on one line.

Instead of paragraphs, poems have **stanzas**. These are groups of lines that explore the same thought or idea. Look at the following stanza from a poem about pigeons.

Pigeons walk down streets and alleys. (line 1)
They live on ledges and roofs.   (line 2)
It's a shock to see   (line 3)
A pigeon in a tree.   (line 4)

One thing people like about poems is their wonderful **imagery**. This means that the words of a poem help you to form a picture in your mind. Read the following stanza.

My heart soars like
A bird in flight
When I see you.
'Cause I love you so

Do you picture a bird flying high? You can picture this from the words in the poem. Can you guess what the word *soars* means from the words around it? It means to "fly high." The second line says *like a bird in flight*.

How It Works

In Lesson 8 you learned about guessing the meaning of words by looking at words around the unknown word. In Lesson 20 you learned about making inferences—figuring out what is not said in words.

Read these four lines of poetry by Emily Dickinson.

> Fame* is a bee.
> It has a song—
> It has a sting—
> Ah, too, it has a wing.

Think about bees. Can you picture a bee in your mind? What do bees do? They buzz. They sting. They fly.

In the poem, fame is compared to a bee. The bee has a song. What can you infer about fame from this? Because a song is a good thing, fame can be a good thing.

The bee has a sting. What inference can you make about fame from this? Because a sting can be painful, fame can be painful.

The bee has a wing. This means that it can fly. Now what can you infer about fame from this? Fame doesn't always last long—it can fly away.

The poem compares fame to a bee.

Try It

How do you feel about arithmetic?

Here are some lines from a poem by Carl Sandburg called "Arithmetic."

> Arithmetic is where numbers fly like pigeons
> in and out of your head.
>
> Arithmetic is where you have to multiply—
> and you carry the multiplication table in your head
> and hope you won't lose it.

What can you infer about how the poet feels about arithmetic? Put a check mark next to the correct answer.

_____ He feels that it is easy to do.

_____ He feels that it's difficult to remember numbers.

_____ He feels that pigeons add better than people.

The poet feels that numbers in arithmetic fly in and out of your head—like pigeons flying around. He also feels that you must hope—that you won't lose (forget) the multiplication tables you have learned. You can infer that the poet finds it difficult to remember numbers.

Practice

First read these two stanzas from the poem "'Hope' is the Thing with Feathers" by Emily Dickinson. Then put a check mark next to the word or words that answer each question that follows.

"Hope" is the thing with feathers
That perches in the soul
And sings the tune without the words,
And never stops at all.

I've heard it in the chilliest land,
And on the strangest sea.
Yet, never, in extremity,*
It asked a crumb of me.

1. What is hope similar to?

_____ a crumb

_____ a bird

_____ a sea

2. What does *perches* mean?

_____ sits

_____ kills

_____ eats

3. Does hope ask for anything?

_____ Yes. It wants bread.

_____ No. Hope doesn't ask for anything.

_____ Yes, but only when it's cold.

Check your answers on page 121.

Follow-Up

Choose one emotion, such as love, hate, hope, or anger. Write one or two sentences comparing the emotion to an animal. Then explain why you chose the animal you did.

Subjects of Poems

What You Know Many songs are about love. Often, a line or two in a song tells you the main idea. Here are four main ideas about love expressed in four different songs:

> My love is like a rose
> A flower that is mine alone.
>
> Love can make you want to die.
>
> Love has a restless mind.
>
> Love is the soul of the world,
> I have lost my heart to it.

Songs—like poems—may be written about any topic, from peace to war, from surfing to climbing. Usually, a line or two in a song or poem gives you the main idea. You get the details as you listen to the entire song or read the entire poem.

How It Works

In Lesson 13 you learned how to find the main idea of a group of sentences. In this lesson you will learn how to find the main idea of a stanza in a poem.

As you did with a group of sentences, first decide what all the details are about. What the details are about is called the **topic**. Then find the most important or the most general point about the topic. This is the **main idea**. All the other information should contain details that support the main idea.

Read the following stanza from a poem called "Harriet Tubman," by Eloise Greenfield. As you read, think about what the topic of the stanza might be.

Harriet Tubman didn't take no stuff
Wasn't scared of nothing neither
Didn't come in this world to be no slave
And wasn't going to stay one either

What is the topic? It's *Harriet Tubman*. She is what all the information in the stanza is about.

What is the main idea of the stanza? *Harriet Tubman wasn't going to stay a slave.*

This is the most important idea. All the details in the stanza support this main idea. Here are the details: *she didn't take no stuff* (she wouldn't put up with things she didn't like), she wasn't scared of anything, and she didn't come into this world to be a slave.

It was a bad time in our history when slavery existed in the United States.

Harriet Tubman made her way to freedom and then helped other slaves do the same.

Try It

Here are two more stanzas from the poem "Harriet Tubman." Read each stanza. Answer the question that follows each stanza.

> "Farewell" she sang to her friends one night
> She was mighty sad to leave 'em
> But she ran away that dark, hot night
> Ran looking for her freedom

What is the topic? _____

Freedom is the topic. What is the most important or the most general statement about freedom? Harriet *ran looking for her freedom*. Other details, such as her saying "Farewell," her sadness about leaving her friends, and her running for freedom on a dark, hot night, support the main idea: She ran looking for freedom.

> She ran to the woods and she ran through the woods
> With the slave catchers right behind her
> And she kept on going till she got to the North
> Where those mean men couldn't find her

What is the topic? _____

Running away is the topic. What is the most general or most important sentence about escaping? *She kept on going till she got to the North.* Details, such as running to and through the woods and the mean slave catchers chasing right behind her, support the main idea—running away to the North.

Practice

Below are three stanzas from a poem called "Western Wagons" by Rosemary and Stephen Vincent Benét. The poem is about pioneers (peye-uh-NEERZ)—people who go somewhere few other people have gone before. The pioneers in this poem went from the east to the west in the United States. They settled in many different places.

Underline the sentence in each stanza that contains the main idea of the stanza.

They went with axe and rifle
when the trail was still to blaze,*
They went with wife and children,
in the prairie schooner* days,
With banjo* and with frying pan—
Susanna, don't you cry!
For I'm off to California
to get rich out there or die!

We've broken land and cleared it,
but we're tired of where we are,
They say that wild Nebraska
is a better place by far.
There's gold in far Wyoming,
there's black earth in Ioway,
So pack up the kids and blankets,
for we're moving out today.

The cowards never started
and the weak died on the road,
And all across the continent*
the endless campfires* glowed.
We'd taken land and settled—
but a traveler passes by
And we're going west tomorrow—
Lordy, never ask us why!

Check your answers on page 121.

Follow-Up

Harriet Tubman ran away so that she could be free. Pioneers moved westward looking for new homes, land, or other reasons. Use what you know from your own life or talk to someone who has moved to the United States from another country. Write a sentence explaining why people come to the United States. Use this as a main idea and write a poem about this.

Rhyme or No Rhyme

What You Know   Have you noticed that most children's poems rhyme? Words **rhyme** when they sound the same. Rhymes make poems easy to remember. Rhymes also make people feel more comfortable with poems. People know what's coming—a word that rhymes with a word they just heard or read. They also know that the word that rhymes falls at the end of a line.

> Little Jack *Horner*
> Sat in a *corner*
> Eating his Christmas *pie*
> He put in his *thumb*
> And pulled out a *plum*
> And said "What a good boy am *I*."

Poems that don't rhyme may "feel" different from poems that do. You may not be comfortable with poems that don't rhyme. Poems that don't rhyme may surprise you, partly because you don't know what's coming.

> The broken window,
> Cracked, in pieces,
> Lets in light
> That is whole.

When you read poems and see how they are alike, you can also see how they are different.

How It Works

You **compare** things to see how they are alike. You **contrast** them to see how they are different. Read the following two poems. The first is a stanza from a poem written from a son to his father. The son tells the father to fight against death, which he refers to as "that good night."

Next are lines from a poem in which a mother tells her son to fight in order to succeed in life.

Poem 1—Stanza

Do not go gentle into that good night,
Old age should burn and rave* at the close of day;
Rage*, rage, against the dying of the light.

Poem 2—Stanza

Don't set you down on the steps
'Cause you find it's kinder hard.
Don't you fall now—
For I'se still goin', honey,
I'se still climbin'
And life for me ain't been no crystal stair.

First, compare these two poems. How are they alike?

These poems are alike because they both offer advice. In the first, a son offers advice to his father. In the second, a mother offers advice to her son.

Also, the main idea in both poems is fighting. In one poem, a person is urged to fight against death. In the other, a person is urged to fight in life in order to succeed.

These poems are different because the first one rhymes and the second one does not. Also, the language in the poems is not similar. In the second example, the language is much more informal, or casual.

Langston Hughes

Dylan Thomas

Langston Hughes and Dylan Thomas were both well-known and highly respected poets.

Try It

Read the two poems below. Then read the questions that follow.
Put a check mark on the answer blank next to the correct answer.

Poem 1

If flowers want to grow
right out of the concrete sidewalk cracks
I'm going to bend down and smell them.

Poem 2

In the morning the city
Spreads its wings
Making a song
In stone that sings

In the evening the city
Goes to bed
Hanging lights
About its head.

1. How are the poems the same?

_____ They both have something to do with a city.

_____ They are both about stone and concrete.

_____ They are both about singing.

The topic of both poems is a city. In one, a person sees a
flower growing through a crack in the sidewalk. In the
other, the poet talks about the city in the morning and
evening.

2. How are the poems different?

_____ Both poems rhyme.

_____ One poem rhymes; one doesn't.

_____ Neither poem rhymes.

The second poem rhymes. The first one doesn't.

Practice

Read these two poems. Then read the questions that follow. Put a check mark next to the correct answer.

Zebra

White as snow.
Black as coal.
Wild and free.
Runs like the wind.

Cat

The black cat yawns,
Opens her jaws,
Stretches her legs,
And shows her claws.

Then she gets up
And stands on four
Long stiff legs
And yawns some more . . .

She lets herself down
With particular care,
And pads away
With her tail in the air.

1. How are the poems similar?

_____ They are both about black animals.

_____ The titles of both poems name an animal.

_____ They both have three stanzas.

2. How are the poems different?

_____ Both poems rhyme.

_____ Neither poem rhymes.

_____ One rhymes; the other doesn't.

Check your answers on page 121.

Follow-Up

Write a poem about an animal.

The Language of Poems

What You Know   You may think that poets use hard or unusual words when they write poems. Although this is sometimes true, it is certainly not always true. Many of the poems in this unit have easy, familiar words.

One of the ways in which language is different in poetry is that words—even easy ones—may mean more than one thing. Also, they may only hint at what is meant rather than coming out and stating the meaning.

For example, in one of the poems in Lesson 21, the poet says, "'Hope' is the thing with feathers." Even though all the words are easy, you have to figure out what this means.

You can read the other lines in the poem and then carefully read the one line you need to figure out. You can also use what you know from your own life. What has feathers? Birds have feathers. You can infer that hope is like a bird.

How It Works

In Lessons 20 and 21 you learned to **make inferences**. You were able to figure out information that is not written. You did this by putting together what was written with what you know from your own life. For example, if you read that red, yellow, and orange leaves are falling from the trees, you might *infer* that it is autumn.

Read this short poem about a common event—buying candy.

> Wandering in the street
> Wanting something sweet
> I went into a store
> And bought some candy.
> It's gone. No more.
> Walking in the street
> Feeling kind of lost
> I dream of something sweet.

Certain details are stated. For example, you learn that the speaker of the poem walked in the street, went into a store, and bought some candy.

Doesn't it sometimes seem as if all the candy you buy just disappears?

What happened to the candy? You know it didn't last. You might infer that the person who bought it ate it. However, you might make other inferences instead. You could infer that someone else ate it or that someone stole it or that the candy got lost.

Remember not to infer more than you should. You know that the person bought candy, but you cannot infer what happened to it, what kind of candy it was, or how much the candy cost.

Try It

Read the following stanza from the poem "Stopping by Woods on a Snowy Evening" by Robert Frost. Then read the inferences that follow. Write yes on the answer blank if you have enough information to make the inference. Write no if you do not.

> Whose woods these are I think I know.
> His house is in the village, though;
> He will not see me stopping here
> To watch his woods fill up with snow.

_____ **1.** It is snowing.

Yes. The speaker of the poem is stopping to watch woods fill up with snow, so it must be snowing.

_____ **2.** The speaker of the poem likes to watch snow fall.

Yes. The speaker is stopping to watch woods fill with snow.

___ **3.** The person who is stopping lives in the village.

No. The person who owns the house lives in the village, but there is no information given about where the person who is stopping lives.

___ **4.** It doesn't snow often in this area.

No. The stanza doesn't say anything about whether or not it snows often.

___ **5.** The speaker of the poem does not own the woods where he is stopping.

Yes. The speaker thinks he knows whose woods they are. If they were his own, he would *know* whose woods they are.

Many poems describe the beauty of nature.

Practice

Read two more stanzas from the poem "Stopping by Woods on a Snowy Evening." Then read the sentences that follow. Write *yes* on the answer blank if you have enough information to make the inference. Write *no* if you do not.

> My little horse must think it queer*
> To stop without a farmhouse near
> Between the woods and frozen lake
> The darkest evening of the year.

___ **1.** The speaker and the horse do not stop often at places in the woods.

___ **2.** They have stopped at farmhouses before.

___ **3.** It is cold out.

___ **4.** It is after midnight.

___ **5.** It is after 5 PM.

> The woods are lovely, dark and deep.
> But I have promises to keep,
> And miles to go before I sleep,
> And miles to go before I sleep.

___ **6.** The speaker doesn't like the woods at night.

___ **7.** The speaker has a long way to go.

___ **8.** The speaker is going home.

___ **9.** The speaker has promised someone he'd be somewhere by a certain time.

Check your answers on page 121.

Follow-Up

Poems use words to suggest other words. Think about the following words about weather: rain, snow, sunshine, heat, cold. Then write a sentence in which another word is used in place of the weather word, for example: *Soft white feathers fall from the sky.*

Kinds of Poems

What You Know Sometimes you want to tell a friend a story. You might tell your friend about the death of someone you both knew. At other times, you might simply want to express strong feelings you have.

If you were to express your story or your feelings in a poem, you might write either a narrative poem or a lyric poem. A **narrative** (NAHR-uh-tihv) **poem** tells a story. A **lyric** (LIHR-ihk) **poem** expresses strong personal emotions, is relatively short, and does not tell a story. Read these two examples and see whether you can tell which one is a narrative poem and which is a lyric poem.

> Beauty is seen
> In the sunlight,
> The trees, the birds,
> Corn growing and people working
> Or dancing for their harvest.
>
> Beauty is heard
> In the night,
> Wind sighing,* rain falling,
> Or a singer chanting*
> Anything in earnest.*

> And he was rich—yes, richer than a king—
> And admirably* schooled in every grace:*
> In fine, we thought he was everything
> To make us wish that we were in his place.
>
> So on we worked, and waited for the light,
> And went without the meat, and cursed the bread;
> And Richard Cory, one calm summer night,
> Went home and put a bullet through his head.

The first poem is a lyric poem. It expresses strong personal emotion. The main idea expressed in the poem is that beauty can be seen or heard almost anywhere. The second example is a narrative poem. It is a story about a man. The poor working people envied Richard Cory because he seemed to have everything, but they didn't really know how he felt or what his life was like.

How It Works

In Lesson 22 you learned to find the main idea in a stanza of poetry. In this lesson, the main idea is not directly stated in the poem. You have to decide what the main idea is. You can do this by reading the poem several times and deciding what the poem is about. This is the main idea. Then find the most important thing the poet says about the main idea. Finally, check that the details support the main idea.

Read the following lyric poem:

Lament*

Listen, children:
Your father is dead.
From his old coats
I'll make you little jackets;
I'll make you little trousers
From his old pants.
There'll be in his pockets
Things he used to put there,
Keys and pennies
Covered with tobacco;
Dan shall have the pennies
To save in his bank;
Anne shall have the keys
To make a pretty noise with.
Life must go on,
And the dead be forgotten;
Life must go on,
Though good men die;
Anne, eat your breakfast;
Dan, take your medicine;
Life must go on;
I forget just why.

What is the main idea expressed in the poem? Circle your choice.

1. The dead often leave things of little value behind.

2. Family life should continue even though the father has died.

3. It's important to tell children about a death in the family.

The correct answer is item 2. The topic of the poem is the father's death. Every detail in the poem supports the main idea that the wife and children need to go on living even though the father's dead. Nothing in the poem talks about how valuable the items are or the importance of discussing death with children.

Try It

Read the following lyric poem. Then put a check mark next to the sentence that sums up the main idea of the poem.

Housecleaning

i always liked house cleaning
even as a child
i dug straightening
the cabinets
putting new paper on
the shelves
washing the refrigerator
inside out
and unfortunately this habit has
carried over and i find
i must remove you
from my life

___ **1.** House cleaning is fun.

___ **2.** House cleaning has become a habit.

___ **3.** One must "house-clean" one's life to keep it in order.

The correct answer is item 3. The poem tells how keeping things orderly is important, both in one's house and in one's personal life.

This woman looks like she is about to do "housecleaning."

Practice

Read the following poem. Put a check mark next to the sentence that sums up the main idea of the poem.

How Heavy the Days

How heavy the days are.
There's not a fire that can warm me,
Not a sun to laugh with me,
Everything bare,
Everything cold and merciless,*
And even the beloved, clear
Stars look desolately* down,
Since I learned in my heart that
Love can die.

___ **1.** The world looks depressing to someone who is no longer loved.

___ **2.** It's a cold winter.

___ **3.** Love is always cruel.

Check your answers on page 121.

Follow-Up

If you were to write a song or poem about the loss of love, what would be the first four lines?

Unit Reviews

Unit 1 Review
Lesson 1

Look at the first vowel in each word below. Write *long* on the answer blank if the vowel is long. Write *short* if the vowel is short.

1. me _____

2. sick _____

3. grow _____

4. sun _____

5. wild _____

6. face _____

Lesson 2

Read these sentences. Some words *begin* with consonant blends. Underline the consonant blends at the beginning of words.

1. Many people from Asia have come to live in the United States.

2. Some flew here in planes.

3. The flight may have lasted over 14 hours.

4. Most people made new friends here.

5. They started new businesses and opened new stores.

Lesson 3

Circle the prefix in each underlined word. Then put a check mark next to the correct meaning of the prefix.

1. Jessica <u>resealed</u> the envelope after she opened it up.

before   again   not

2. Some people say that Friday the thirteenth is an <u>unlucky</u> day.

before   wrong   not

3. The <u>pregame</u> show featured clowns, acrobats, and jugglers.

before   not   again

Lesson 4

Read the following sentences and look at the underlined words.
Then answer the questions that follow each group of sentences.

1. Harry just got a small dog. It is so <u>tiny</u> that it can fit under the couch. There isn't room for a <u>big</u> dog in his house.

   a. Which word is a synonym for *small*? _____

   b. Which word is an antonym for *small*? _____

2. Katherine was given a very valuable ring by her mother. To her, it was <u>priceless</u>. All her other jewelry seemed <u>cheap</u> by comparison.

   a. Which word is a synonym for *valuable*? _____

   b. Which word is an antonym for *valuable*? _____

Lesson 5

Read these sentences. Some words *end* in consonant blends.
Write these words in the answer blanks. Then circle the
consonant blends in the words you have written.

1. A dangerous storm can do a lot of harm. _____ _____

2. A bolt of lightning can hit a tree and seriously hurt a person.

   _____ _____ _____

3. An entire forest can be destroyed. _____

Answers for Unit 1 Review begin on page 121.

Unit 2 Review
Lesson 6

Write each underlined word on one of the long answer blanks.
Look at the first vowel in the word. Write *long* on the short
answer blank if the word has a long vowel sound. Write *short* on
the short answer blank if the vowel has a short vowel sound.

1. In a <u>desert</u>, food and water are hard to <u>find</u>.

   _____ _____ _____ _____

2. <u>Most</u> deserts are extremely <u>hot</u> during the day.

   _____ _____ _____ _____

Lesson 7

Read the sentences below. Look at the underlined words.
Choose the suffix that best fits the meaning. Write the suffix in
the space provided on the underline.

1. Some people are perfect_____ happy in the summer.

    ly   er   ful   less

2. A summer vacation_____ loves to go to the beach.

    ly   er   ful   less

3. Warm sand and beautiful ocean breezes make them thank_____ to be alive.

    ly   er   ful   less

Lesson 8

Read the sentences below. Then figure out what the underlined
word in each sentence means. Write the meaning of this word
on the answer blank.

1. Many people like to collect things. They underline{accumulate} as many baseball
cards or comic books or even ticket stubs as they can. Often these people
can't find enough room for all the things they have.

What does *accumulate* mean?

_____

2. Some things that people collect are unique. They have to look in small
stores and flea markets to find these objects.

What does *unique* mean?

_____

Lesson 9

Read these sentences. Then answer the questions.

Amy Tan's book *The Kitchen God's Wife* was published in 1991. It has received many awards and has been read by thousands of people all over the world. The book is about Winnie and her daughter Pearl and the secrets Winnie tells her daughter. Winnie tells Pearl about life outside the city of Shanghai, China, in the 1920s. She also tells her about life in China during World War II. She tells a very sad story about her arrival in the United States in 1949.

The book is beautifully written. You will not be able to put it down.

1. When did Winnie arrive in the United States?

_____

2. Who is the author of this book?

_____

3. What city in China does Winnie tell about?

_____

Lesson 10

Read the following sentences and look at the underlined words. Then answer the questions that follow each group of sentences.

1. Do you <u>enjoy</u> listening to music? Many people like to listen to good musicians. They hate hearing musicians who aren't well-trained.

  a. Which word is a synonym for *enjoy*? _____

  b. Which word is an antonym for *enjoy*? _____

2. Some people like to hear music that is <u>loud</u>. The thunderous sounds please them. Other people prefer music to be soft.

  a. Which word is a synonym for *loud*? _____

  b. Which word is an antonym for *loud*? _____

Answers for Unit 2 Review begin on page 122.

Unit 3 Review
Lesson 11

Read this paragraph and then answer the questions that follow.

At 9:00 P.M., the sound of the first fireworks could be heard. We were sitting in Locust Valley Park. As we looked up, we saw the most beautiful sight. The sky looked as if it were raining diamonds and rubies.

1. What sound was heard? _____

2. Where were the people? _____

3. What did the fireworks look like? _____

Lesson 12

Read the following sentences. Write F in the answer blank if the sentence is a fact. Write O if the sentence is an opinion.

_____ **1.** California is a state in the United States.

_____ **2.** California is the best state to live in.

_____ **3.** The capital of California is Sacramento.

_____ **4.** More than 29 million people live in California.

_____ **5.** Hollywood is the best place to visit.

Lesson 13

Read this paragraph and find the main idea.

"Jim, darling," she cried, "don't look at me that way. I had my hair cut off and sold it because I couldn't have lived through Christmas without giving you a present. It'll grow out again—you won't mind, will you? I just had to do it. My hair grows awfully fast. Say "Merry Christmas!" Jim, and let's be happy. You don't know what a nice—what a beautiful, nice gift I've got for you."

Put a check mark next to the main idea.

_____ My hair grows awfully fast.
_____ I cut my hair cut off and sold it because I couldn't have lived through Christmas without giving you a present.
_____ Say "Merry Christmas!" Jim, and let's be happy.

Lesson 14

Read this paragraph. Then number the steps in the order in which they took place.

The alarm clock sounded. Victor immediately got out of bed. He walked to the bathroom, brushed his teeth, and washed his face. He took his suit and shirt out of the closet and dressed quickly. He raced out the door without eating breakfast.

_____ He walked to the bathroom, brushed his teeth, and washed his face.

_____ He raced out of the door without eating breakfast.

_____ The alarm clock sounded.

_____ He took his suit and shirt out of the closet and dressed quickly.

_____ Victor immediately got out of bed.

Lesson 15

Read each sentence below. Then put a check mark next to the cause that leads to the effect.

1. Effect: Jennie buys a wedding dress.

   Cause: _____ She works in a bridal shop.
   _____ She is getting married.
   _____ She is graduating from high school.

2. Effect: Ira and Jennie have hired a moving van.

   Cause: _____ They are getting married.
   _____ They hope to find a place to live.
   _____ They are moving to a new apartment.

Answers for Unit 3 Review begin on page 122.

Unit 4 Review
Lesson 16

Write F in the answer blank if the sentence is a fact. Write O if the sentence is an opinion.

_____ **1.** The Earth is a planet.

_____ **2.** Pluto is the smallest planet.

_____ **3.** Saturn's rings make Saturn the most beautiful planet.

Lesson 17

Read the sentences below. Put a check mark next to the one that contains the main idea.

_____ **1.** Greta works out every day for two hours.

_____ **2.** Greta swims whenever she gets the chance.

_____ **3.** Greta loves sports.

_____ **4.** Greta plays in a weekly basketball game.

_____ **5.** On weekends, Greta plays volleyball with her friends.

Lesson 18

Put a check mark next to the effect that results from the cause.

Cause: Ten inches of rain have fallen in one hour.

Effect: _____ It is summer.
_____ Clouds appear in the sky.
_____ The city's streets are flooded.

Lesson 19

Read both paragraphs. Then put a check mark next to the correct answer.

The play takes place in the 1990s in Boston, Massachusetts. All the action occurs on an outdoor basketball court.

The setting of the play is in Houston, Texas. It takes place outdoors in 1991, on the porch of a very large house.

1. Both settings are

_____ a. indoors.
_____ b. outdoors.
_____ c. about basketball.

2. One difference between the two settings is that

_____ a. one takes place in Massachusetts; the other is in Texas.
_____ b. one takes place indoors, and the other takes place outdoors.
_____ c. one takes place in the 1990s, and the other takes place at an earlier time.

Lesson 20

First read the following information. Then read the sentences below. Write *yes* on the answer blank if you can make the inferences. Write *no* if you cannot.

Two strange-looking "people" walk out of a spaceship that has just landed in my front yard. They have wires sticking out of their heads. They each have four eyes and no ears. They are green. When they see us, they jump up and down.

_____ **1.** The people are from Mars.

_____ **2.** They have just landed on Earth.

_____ **3.** These people are cruel.

_____ **4.** The people are glad to be on Earth.

Answers for Unit 4 Review begin on page 123.

Unit 5 Review
Lesson 21

Read these lines of poetry. Then put a check mark next to the word or words that answer each question that follows.

Had my father, my grandfather, and his,
had they been asked whether I would ever see snow,
They certainly—in another language—
would have answered,
no. Seeing snow for me
will always mean a slight or not so slight
suspension* of the laws of nature.
I was not born to see snow.
I was not meant to see snow.
Even now, snowbound as I've been all these years,
my surprise does not subside . . .
Where I come from, you know,
it's never snowed:
not once, not ever, not yet.

1. What has caused the poet to be so surprised?

_____ his grandfather _____ seeing snow _____ a house

2. What does subside mean?

_____ get bigger _____ seem funny _____ get less

Lesson 22

Read the following poem. Underline the three lines that contain the main idea of this poem.

> There are some millionaires
> With money they can't use
> Their wives run round like banshees*
> Their children sing the blues
> They've got expensive doctors
> To cure their hearts of stone.
> But nobody
> No nobody
> Can make it out there alone.

Lesson 23

Read these lines of poetry from two different poems. Then read the questions that follow. Put a check mark next to the right answer.

> My own dear love he is strong and bold
> And he cares not what comes after.
> His words ring sweet as a chime* of gold
> And his eyes are lit with laughter.
> He is jubilant* as a flag unfurled*—
> Oh, a girl, she'd not forget him.
> My own dear love, he is all my world—
> And I wish I'd never met him.

> I love bright words, words up and singing early;
> Words that are luminous* in the dark, and sing;
> Warm lazy words, white cattle under trees;
> I love words opalescent,* cool, and pearly,*
> Like midsummer moths, and honeyed words like bees,
> Gilded* and sticky, with a little sting.

1. How are the poems similar?

_____ They are both about falling in love.
_____ Both rhyme.
_____ Both are about mothers and their children.

2. How are the poems different?

_____ One poem is about a man and a woman; the other is about words.
_____ One rhymes; the other does not.
_____ In one poem, the speaker is angry; in the other, the speaker is sad.

Lesson 24

Read this poem by Robert Frost called "House Fear" and the sentences that follow it. Write *yes* on the blank if you have enough information to make the inference. Write *no* if you do not.

Always—I tell you this they learned—
Always at night when they returned
To the lonely house from far away
To lamps unlighted and fire gone gray,
They learned to rattle the lock and key
To give whatever might chance to be
Warning and time to be off in flight:
And preferring the out- to the in-door night
They learned to leave the house door wide
Until they had lit the lamp inside.

1. The people in the poem sometimes leave their home. _____

2. When they return, they are careful before entering their house.

   _____

3. Many burglars have robbed their home. _____

4. They turn off their lamps before they go away. _____

Lesson 25

Read the following poem. Underline the sentence that sums up its main idea.

If There Be Sorrow
If there be sorrow
let it be
for things undone
undreamed
unrealized*
unattained*
to these add one:
Love withheld . . .
. . . restrained*

1. It's silly to feel sorrow when one can just as easily feel happiness.

2. The greatest cause of sorrow is holding back your love.

3. You should dream, and your dreams will come true.

Answers for Unit 5 Review begin on page 123.

Word List

The words here are listed in **alphabetical order**. This means that they are listed in the order of the letters of the alphabet. To find the word you are looking for, follow these steps:

1. Look at the first letter of the word you need to find. Then find this letter in the listing that follows. For example, if you are looking up the word *sighing*, you would look under the letter *S*.

2. Once you have found the first letter of the word, look at the second letter. The second letter of the word *sighing* is *i*. Look through the words listed under *S*. Words that begin with *sa*; *sc*; and *sh* come before the word *sighing* because the letters *a*, *c*, and *h*, come before the letter *i* in the alphabet. For example, the word *shabby* comes before the word *sighing* because *sh* comes before *si*.

3. If the first two letters of the word you are looking up are the same as in other words listed, look at the third letter. The third letter in the word *shabby* is *a*, which is the first letter of the alphabet. This means that *shabby* is probably the first word listed under *sh*.

A
admirably (AHD-mihr-uh-blee)   Very well or excellently
attic (AT-ihk)   A small room directly under the roof of a house, often used for storage

B
banjo (BAN-joh)   A musical instrument similar to a guitar
banshees (BAN-sheez)   In Irish folk stories, ghostlike women who appear to a family to give a warning that one of them will soon die. When they appear, banshees make loud crying noises
blaze a trail (BLAYZ uh TRAYL)   To lead or be the first to go somewhere or do something

C
campfire (KAMP-FEYER)   An outdoor fire at a camp, where people are spending time in the woods or on a hike
chanting (CHAHN-tihng)   Singing
character (KAYR-ihk-tuhr)   A person in a story. The main character is the most important person in the story.
charming (CHAHR-ming)   Pleasing and likable

chime (CHEYEM)   To ring, like church bells

clogs (KLAHGZ)   Shoes with thick, wooden soles

concentration camps (KOHN-sehn-TRAY-shun KAMPS)   A place like a prison. During World War II millions of innocent people were sent to concentration camps in Europe, where they were forced to work, starved, and died or were killed. The lives of 9 to 10 million people ended in concentration camps.

content (kuhn-TIHNT)   Pleased or satisfied

continent (KAHN-tih-nehnt)   A large mass of land usually made up of countries; for example, Canada, the United States, and Mexico are countries in the continent of North America

cramped (KRAMPT)   Little room to move around in, as in a small house or apartment

cremate (KREE-mayt)   To burn a dead body to ashes

D

desolately (DEHS-uh-luht-lee)   Sadly; without warmth, comfort, or hope

dozed (DOHZD)   Slept lightly

Dutch (DUHCH)   Relating to people or things from the Netherlands (Holland)

E

earnest (ERN-ehst)   Serious (In earnest means "seriously.")

enormous (ee-NOHR-muhs)   Very large

exposes (ehks-POHZEZ)   Reveals or makes known

extremity (ehks-TREHM-ih-tee)   A situation in which things are at their most serious or at their worst

F

fitfully (FIHT-fuhl-lee)   On and off; doing something, then stopping, then starting again, and so on

fond of (FAHND UHV)   Like to, for example, to be fond of dancing means that one likes to dance

G

gilded (GIHL-dihd)   Covered with a thin layer of gold

goggles (GAH-guhlz)   Special glasses that are worn to protect the eyes

grace (GRAYS)   Pleasing actions and good manners

grazing (GRAYZ ihng)   Eating grass; animals such as cows, zebras, deer, and horses walk around in fields grazing.

H

hitchhiker (HIHCH-heyek-uhr)   A person who travels by trying to get rides from passing cars

Holland (HAHL-uhnd)   A country in northwestern Europe; another name for Holland is the Netherlands.

I

in spite of (IHN SPEYET UHV)   Regardless; even though

J

jubilant (JOO-buh-luhnt)   Joyful and full of triumph
jurisdiction (jur-ihs-DIHK-shuhn)   The right or power to control something

L

lament (luh-MEHNT)   A statement of mourning or grief
lift (LIHFT)   A ride in a car
literally (LIHT-uhr-uh-lee)   Relating to the true meaning of a word; for
    example, if someone says that he or she could faint, this person could in
    fact pass out and is not pretending.
luminous (LOO-mihn-uhs)   Giving off light; bright or shining

M

massacred (MAHS-uh-kuhrd)   Totally destroyed or killed
merciless (MUHR-sih-lehs)   Without mercy or pity
mob (MAHB)   A crowd of people who may be angry, shouting, and
    throwing things; the police are often needed to control a mob.
mystery (MIHS-tuhr-ee)   A story in which a crime is usually committed and
    the person who committed the crime is not known until the end.

N

nasty (NAHS-tee)   Mean, unkind, rude, and unpleasant
Nazis (NAHTS-eez)   Members of a political party in Germany before and
    during World War II. One belief of the Nazi party was that people who
    did not have the same religion, race, or ethnic background as the Nazis
    should not be allowed to live among the Nazis. The Nazis sent millions
    of these people to concentration camps where they died or were killed.
Netherlands (NEH-thur-lundz)   A country in northwestern Europe; another
    name for the Netherlands is Holland.

O

opalescent (o-puh-LEHS-uhnt)   Shining with a light of many colors.

P

pangs (PANGZ)   Short, sharp pains that happen suddenly
pearly (PUHR-lee)   Looking like or shining like a pearl
pecking at (PEHK-ihng-AT)   Picking on or nagging at
peculiar (puh-KYOOL-yuhr)   Unusual or odd
prairie schooner (PREHR-ee SKOON-uhr)   A covered wagon used by
    pioneers to travel across North America

Pueblo (PWEHB-loh)   Certain Native American people of the southwestern United States; Pueblo is also a city in the state of Colorado.

puzzled (PUHZ-uld)   Confused by a problem that is difficult to solve

Q

queer (KWEER)   Unusual or odd

R

ratty-faced (RAT-ee FAYST)   Having a face that looks like the face of a rat

rage (RAYG)   To talk in an angry, violent way

rave (RAYV)   To talk in a wild, crazy way

restrained (re-STRAYND)   Controlled in expressing feelings or thoughts

review (ree-VYOO)   (1) To review: To see or read something and form and opinion about it. (2) A review: An opinion formed after seeing or reading something; usually the opinion is expressed in writing.

reviewer (ree-VYOO-uhr)   A person who reviews something; this person may work for a newspaper, magazine, or TV show.

S

shabby (SHAB-bee)   Not in good condition because of being worn or used too much; an old sweater or an old house might be described as shabby.

shielded (SHEEL-dihd)   Protected

sighing (SEYE-ihng)   The sound of wind, or breath, moving gently

splattered (SPLAT-tuhrd)   Splashed

suspect (SUHS-pect)   A person who is thought to have committed a crime; this person may or may not be arrested, guilty, or in jail.

suspense (suh-SPEHNS)   A kind of excitement in a movie, book, or play that results when no one knows how the story will turn out.

suspension (suh-SPEHN-shuhn)   The stopping of something

T

thumbing (THUHM-ing)   The action used by hitchhikers of putting the hand out with the thumb pointing in the direction the hitchhiker wants to go.

U

unattained (uhn-uh-TAYND)   Not gotten or done

unfurled (uhn-FUHRLD)   Opened or unfolded

unrealized (uhn-REE-uh-leyezd)   Did not come true or become real

up-tempo (UHP TEHM-poh)   In music, a fast-moving beat

W

withheld (wihth-HEHLD)   Held back; not given

wreckage (REHK-ihg)   What is left after something has been ruined or destroyed

Answers

Unit 1 Nonfiction

LESSON 1

Practice

1. is   short
2. no   long
3. led   short
4. time   long

5. children   short
6. see   long
7. find   long

LESSON 2

Practice

1. pretty smile
4. stories, space

2. traveled, from, States
5. proud, cry

3. *Street*

LESSON 3

Practice

1. misunderstand: wrong
3. preset: before

2. unlike: not
4. nonstop: not

LESSON 4

Practice

1. a. depressing
   b. cheerful
2. a. silent
   b. noisy
3. a. hard
   b. easy

LESSON 5

Practice

1. eve(nt), intere(st)
3. wo(rk), cartooni(st)

2. differe(nt), be(st)
4. Importa(nt), fro(nt)

Unit 2 *Commentary on the Arts*

LESSON 6
Practice

1. television: short   live: long   jazz: short
2. can: short   current: short   events: long
3. adventure: short   old: long   from: short
4. reviewers: long   in: short   magazines: short
5. write: long   acting: short   about: short

LESSON 7
Practice

1. performers   2. thankful   3. fearful   4. calmly
5. hopeless   6. loudly

LESSON 8
Practice

1. perfect   2. dangerous

LESSON 9
Practice

1. In Central Park, New York City
2. Patricia D. Cornwell
3. She believes all the details in her books should be as realistic as possible.

LESSON 10
Practice

1. a. penniless   2. a. plenty   3. a. recall
   b. rich   b. little   b. forget

Unit 3 *Fiction*

LESSON 11
Practice

1. The paragraph is written from the first-person point of view.
2. To a bad place (hell)
3. He wanted a change.
4. She "got mad"—she got angry.
5. After dinner
6. She was her sister.

LESSON 12

Practice

1. F Tony Hillerman was once president of the Mystery Writers of America. (This can be checked in the records.)
2. F He has received the Edgar and Grand Masters Awards. (This can be checked in the records.)
3. O His characters are the most interesting characters in suspense novels. (The word *most* suggests a value.)
4. F Hillerman has written *Coyote Waits*, *Talking God*, and *A Thief in Time*, among other books. (You can find these books and see that he wrote them.)
5. O His best book is *Dance Hall of the Dead*. (The word *best* suggests a value.)
6. F In Hillerman's books, Officer Jim Chee and Lieutenant Joe Leaphorn are part of the Navajo Tribal Police. (You can look in the books to check this.)
7. F A bullet kills Officer Jim Chee's friend Del, in the novel *Coyote Waits*. (You can look in the book to check this.)
8. O Del was one of the nicest guys a person could know. (One person might think this; others might not.)
9. O Nobody writes a better suspense novel than Tony Hillerman. (The word *better* suggests a value.)
10. O Leaphorn and Chee solve the hardest cases. (Some people might agree; others might not.)

LESSON 13

Practice

The main idea is: Maybe the baby is sick.

LESSON 14

Practice

5 Men poured gasoline over his clothes.
3 He put on goggles.
1 He pulled on his boots and gloves.
4 He plugged his nose and ears with cotton.
2 He stuffed the spaces between his boots and gloves with gasoline-soaked rags.

LESSON 15

Practice

1. He doesn't want to disturb his father.　　2. The son is curious.
3. The father doesn't like the light.

Unit 4 Drama

LESSON 16

Practice

1. F
2. O Karl says "He wasn't a big dog," but he also says he dug the hole up to his knees, a hole that could hold a quite large dog.
3. O Marsha says "I feel old," but no age is given or suggested for her or Karl.
4. F
5. F

LESSON 17

Practice

The main idea is number 4: I mean you be surprised, it don't have to be him. All of Eddie's statements give Catherine reasons for not choosing "him."

LESSON 18

Practice

1. He practices football as much as he can.
2. Troy tries to talk his son out of playing football.

LESSON 19

Practice

1. b. outdoors, on a roof
2. b. One takes place on the roof of a tall building, and the other takes place on the roof of a small building.

LESSON 20

Practice

1. Yes. The fact that the man is carrying a big stick in one hand and a dead rabbit in the other hand suggests that he has killed the rabbit.
2. Yes. The man lives in a hole in the mountain; both he and the woman have long, messy hair and wear only a few, dirty clothes.
3. No. We cannot tell whether the people are living in the present or in the past. Their dress or hair style might belong to people thousands of years ago or belong to people at the present time who live in hard conditions away from any town.
4. No.
5. No.

Unit 5 Poetry

LESSON 21

Practice

1. a bird; Hope is called "a thing with feathers" that sings.
2. sits
3. No. The poet says that Hope "never asked a crumb of me."

LESSON 22

Practice

Stanza 1. For I'm off to California
to get rich out there or die!
Stanza 2. So pack up the kids and blankets,
for we're moving out today.
Stanza 3. And we're going west tomorrow —
Lordy, never ask us why!

LESSON 23

Practice

1. The titles of both poems name an animal.
2. One rhymes; the other doesn't.

LESSON 24

Practice

1. Yes. You can infer they do not stop often at places in the woods because the horse thinks it queer when they do.
2. Yes. The horse thinks it is queer when they stop "without a farmhouse near"; it expects to stop at farmhouses.
3. Yes.   **4.** No.   **5.** No.
6. No. The speaker says the woods are "lovely," and stops to watch them fill up with snow.
7. Yes.   **8.** No.   **9.** No. His "promises" are not specific.

LESSON 25

Practice

1. The world looks depressing to someone who is no longer loved.

Unit 1 Review

LESSON 1

1. me: long   **2.** sick: short   **3.** grow: long   **4.** sun: short
5. wild: long   **6.** face: long

LESSON 2

1. from   **2.** flew, planes   **3.** flight   **4.** friends
5. started, stores

LESSON 3

1. <u>re</u>sealed: again; **2.** <u>un</u>lucky: not;   **3.** <u>pre</u>game: before

LESSON 4

1. a. tiny; b. big   **2.** a. priceless; b. cheap

LESSON 5

1. sto(rm), ha(rm); **2.** bo(lt), hu(rt);   **3.** fore(st)

Unit 2 Review

LESSON 6

1. d<u>e</u>sert: short; f<u>i</u>nd: long   **2.** m<u>o</u>st: long; h<u>o</u>t: short

LESSON 7

1. perfect<u>ly</u>   **2.** vacation<u>er</u>   **3.** thank<u>ful</u>

LESSON 8

1. collect, or pile up   **2.** one of a kind

LESSON 9

1. 1949   **2.** Amy Tan   **3.** Shanghai

LESSON 10

1. a. like; b. hate **2.** a. thunderous; b. soft

Unit 3 Review

LESSON 11

1. the sound of fireworks   **2.** in Locust Valley Park
3. as if it were raining diamonds and rubies

LESSON 12

1. F   **2.** O   **3.** F   **4.** F
5. F

LESSON 13

The main idea is: I had my hair cut off and sold it because I couldn't have lived through Christmas without giving you a present.

LESSON 14

3 He walked to the bathroom, brushed his teeth, and washed his face.
5 He raced out of the door without eating breakfast.
1 The alarm clock sounded.
4 He took his suit and shirt out of the closet and dressed quickly.
2 Victor immediately got out of bed.

LESSON 15

1. She is getting married.
2. They are moving to a new apartment.

Unit 4 Review

LESSON 16

1. F   **2.** F   **3.** O

LESSON 17

3. Greta loves sports.

LESSON 18

The city's streets are flooded.

LESSON 19

1. b. outdoors
2. a. one takes place in Massachusetts, and the other takes place in Texas.

LESSON 20

1. No   **2.** Yes   **3.** No   **4.** No

Unit 5 Review

LESSON 21

1. seeing snow   **2.** get less

LESSON 22

But nobody
No nobody
Can make it out there alone.

LESSON 23

1. Both rhyme.
2. One poem is about a man and a woman; the other is about words.

LESSON 24

1. Yes   **2.** Yes   **3.** No   **4.** Yes

LESSON 25

1. The greatest cause of sorrow is holding back your love.

(continued from page ii)

Greenfield. © 1978 by Eloise Greenfield. Selection reprinted by permission of HarperCollins Publishers. "Western Wagons" by Rosemary and Stephen Vincent Benet from A BOOK OF AMERICANS by Rosemary and Stephen Vincent Benet Copyright 1933 by Rosemary and Stephen Vincent Benet. Copyright renewed (c) 1964 by Thomas C. Benet, Stephanie B. Mahin, and Rachel Lewis Benet. All rights reserved. Reprinted by permission of Brandt & Brandt Literary Agents, Inc. "Do Not Go Gentle Into That Good Night" by Dylan Thomas from THE POEMS OF DYLAN THOMAS. Copyright ©1952 by Dylan Thomas. Reprinted by permission of New Directions Publishing Corp. "Mother to Son" by Langston Hughes from SELECTED POEMS by Langston Hughes. Copyright 1926 by Alfred A. Knopf, Inc. and renewed 1954 by Langston Hughes. Reprinted by permission of the publisher. "The City" by David Ignatow, "The City" from POEMS 1934-1969, ©1970 by David Ignatow, Wesleyan University Press by permission of the University Press of New England. "City" by Langston Hughes from COLLECTED POEMS by Langston Hughes. Copyright ©1994 by the Estate of Langston Hughes. Reprinted by permission of Alfred A. Knopf, Inc. "Cat" by Mary Britton Miller from MENAGERIE by Mary Britton Miller. Reprinted by permission of James N. Miller. "Stopping by Woods on a Snowy Evening" by Robert Frost from THE POETRY OF ROBERT FROST edited by Edward Connery Lathem. Copyright 1951 by Robert Frost. Copyright 1923 ©1969 by Henry Holt and Co., Inc. Reprinted by permission of Henry Holt and Co. "Beauty" by E-Yeh-Shure from I AM A PUEBLO INDIAN GIRL by E-Yeh-Shure. Copyright © 1939 by William Morrow and Company, Inc. Copyright renewed 1967 by Louise Abeita Chiwiwi. By permission of William Morrow and Company, Inc. "Richard Cory" by Edward Arlington Robinson. Public Domain. "Richard Cory" from THE CHILDREN OF NIGHT by Edward Arlington Robinson, published by Charles Scribner's Sons. "Lament" by Edna St. Vincent Millay. From COLLECTED POEMS, HarperCollins. Copyright 1921, 1948 by Edna St. Vincent Millay. Reprinted by permission of Elizabeth Barnett, literary executor. "Housecleaning" by Nikki Giovanni from THE WOMEN AND THE MEN by Nikki Giovanni. Copyright © 1970, 1974, 1975 by Nikki Giovanni. By permission of William Morrow and Company, Inc. "How Heavy the Days..." by Hermann Hesse from POEMS by Hermann Hesse, selected and translated by James Wright. Translation copyright ©1970 by James Wright. Reprinted by permission of Farrar, Straus & Giroux, Inc. "Seeing Snow" by Gustavo Perez Firmat from BILINGUAL BLUES (1995). Reprinted by permission of The Bilingual Press/Editorial Bilingue, Arizona State University, Tempe, AZ. "Alone" by Maya Angelou from OH PRAY MY WINGS ARE GONNA FIT ME WELL by Maya Angelou. Copyright ©1975 by Maya Angelou Reprinted by permission of Random House Inc. "Love Song" by Dorothy Parker. Copyright 1926, renewed ©1954 by Dorothy Parker, from THE PORTABLE DOROTHY PARKER by Dorothy Parker, introduction by Brendan Gill. Used by permission of Viking Penguin, a division of Penguin Books USA Inc. "Pretty Words" by Elinor Wylie from Collected Poems by Elinor Wylie. Copyright ©1932 by Alfred A. Knopf, Inc. Renewed 1960 by Edwina C. Rubenstein. Reprinted by permission of the publishers. "House Fear" by Robert Frost. Public Domain. "House Fear" from THE POETRY OF ROBERT FROST, edited by Edward Connery Lathem. Copyright 1916. ©1969 by Holt, Rinehart and Winston. "If There By Sorrow" by Mari Evans from I AM A BLACK WOMAN by Mari Evans, published by William Morrow & Co. Copyright ©1970 by Mari Evans. Reprinted by permission of the author.